CW01464380

Travel

for Your

Life

How to quit your job, travel the world,
and transform your life

Plus essential travelling tips, from staying safe to
making the most of your trip

Chantell Glenville

Lifestyles
P R E S S

Published by Lifestyles Press
14 St. John's Road, Tunbridge Wells, TN4 9NP
United Kingdom

ISBN-13: 978-0-9935431-4-2

To all those who dream they could travel.
You can and you will.

"If you can dream it, you can do it."
Walt Disney

"To dream by night is to escape your life. To dream by day is to make it happen."
Stephen Richards

Contents

Introduction

I quit my job in 2014 to travel and it's one of the best decisions I've ever made.

It took me a long time to make the decision, though, with a lot of worries about how I'd afford it, what would happen to my career, whether it would be safe to go alone, and a hundred other concerns that played on my mind.

This book is written for those of you who'd love to take off and travel but are also fighting these dilemmas. It gives practical advice on how to overcome them, explains why it is so worthwhile to make the decision to travel, and gives suggestions on safety, planning, and attitude for once you start the journey.

This is not a guide book that provides information on multiple destinations. It is instead a book on *why* you should travel and *how* to do it.

Travel is genuinely one of the best things you can do in your life, and if this book encourages even just one other person to travel, writing it has been 100% worth it.

Part 1

Let's Go

Chapter 1

The Time Is Now

"A real decision is measured by the fact that you've taken a new action. If there's no action, you haven't truly decided.... The most important thing you can do to achieve your goals is to make sure that as soon as you set them, you immediately begin to create momentum."
Tony Robbins

"Once you make a decision, the universe conspires to make it happen."
Ralph Waldo Emerson

If you have ever had an urge to travel, the time to do it is now.

You may think that's easier said than done and there are a multitude of reasons why you can't travel right now, but they *aren't* reasons not to do it. They're just the things that you have to start working to overcome from this moment on. The time to make the firm decision that you *will* travel and start getting your life in order so that you are able to go is *now*.

The first step to any action is decision. Make the decision and then start taking steps towards achieving it, no matter how small those steps are. If you keep making steps, big or small, you'll eventually get there.

"A journey of 1,000 miles starts with the first step."
Lao-Tsé

If it isn't quite the right time for you to travel immediately, take this opportunity to fix any obstacles that are making travel hard for you.

Bear in mind, though, that there will probably never be a perfect time to travel. There will always be one reason or another that you can give yourself as to why it's not the right time to go.

Since that will always be the case, don't let the excuses win out.

I know so many people who didn't travel at various points in their lives because "the time wasn't right". They found in hindsight that the reasons that stopped them weren't that important or insurmountable. If they'd just made the decision, kept to it, and started working towards it, they would have been able to travel without any detrimental effect on their lives.

Instead, 10 or 15 years on, they still haven't lived out their travel dreams.

For example, one of my friends wanted to take a year after university to travel but then found what he thought was his dream job, so stayed. He is now 34, and only two years ago did he first manage to take a few weeks off to travel because he got so wrapped up in the cycle of working and going from one job to another. He still wants to travel long-term and has finally made the decision to do so, but it has taken 13 years. He freely admits that he should have done it years ago. None of the reasons that stopped him before were barriers he couldn't have overcome. And the "perfect job" turned out to not be so perfect in the end.

Another friend has been saying for the last 12 years that she wants to get a working holiday visa for Australia and live there for a year, but has never done anything about it. She says, "I don't have enough money in my bank account to get the visa",[1] but she's never tried to change that situation.

Had she decided four years ago that the time is now, and that she would definitely go to Australia, she could have been putting aside £1.75 ($2.50)[2] a day for that time and would now have the money. No one will miss £1.75 a day unless they are genuinely on the bread line. And if you are, you just need to find another way to fund the travel, such as finding a company to sponsor you[3] or working as you go.

This friend, who's dreamed of working in Australia for 12 years but never actually made the decision to do it, is now about to turn 31. You have to apply for

---

[1] The Australian government requires you to have at least $5000 AUD, around £2500 GBP or $3700 USD, in the bank to get a working holiday visa if you're from the UK.

[2] All dollar amounts in this book are USD, unless otherwise noted. For up-to-the-minute currency conversion rates, see www.xe.com.

[3] In Australia companies may sponsor "highly skilled workers" for a permanent visa to work in their businesses. For more information on visas for Australia, visit www.border.gov.au. Sponsored visas are also available for many other countries.

the work visa before you are 31 years old, therefore she has now missed that opportunity for good. Missing out on something she really wanted to do just doesn't seem worth £1.75 a day. It's money that could easily have been saved by going out one less night a week or taking packed lunches to work for example.

I'm not telling you these stories to make you depressed and think, "S**t, I've missed my chance". I'm telling you this because whatever stage of life you are now in, *you have not missed your chance*, you can still do it, but the time to start is *now*.

You might have to be flexible about what your dreams are, if there is an age restriction on where you want to go or the like, and you may have a more complex web of obstacles to work round before you can go, but hey, that's part of the journey too. Overcoming the obstacles will make it so much more fulfilling when you do get there.

And you *will* get there.

Chapter 2

How to Convince Your-
self the Time Is Now

"Protect the downside by working out what the worst possible consequences would be, then deciding whether to accept."
Richard Branson

When making hard decisions it's common to make lists of the pros and cons of each action, but do you actually need to know all the pros if it's something that you *really* want to do? Chances are you've already worked out all the advantages and know that it's an activity you'd enjoy. The thing holding you back from the decision is likely the cons; the obstacles you think are standing in your way and the risks you perceive to be attached to the action.

So instead of writing a pros and cons lists, take 30 minutes and write two lists that are focused on the cons and their solutions instead.

First make a list of the obstacles that are stopping you from leaving right now, whether that is insufficient funds, a mortgage to pay, or other commitments. Now spend some time thinking of how you could overcome each obstacle. Write out these possible solutions next to each item and start taking action to solve them, right now.[4]

This is your **Obstacles List**.

Next write a list of the worst-case scenarios that could occur as a result of your travels. This worst-case scenario list focuses on the negatives, but again instead of just jotting down the drawbacks of the decision, list as many solutions as you can think of, too.

This second list is an idea that comes from Tim Ferriss, author of *The 4-Hour Work Week*, who suggests, like Branson above, that we need to define our fears in order to overcome them.[5]

When making the decision to travel for an extended period of time, for example, some of the worst-case scenarios could be things like:

- run out of money in Outer Mongolia
- fall off the career ladder at home

---

[4] See Chapter 4 for how to overcome the two specific challenges mentioned above.

[5] Tim Ferriss's method for doing this also includes the probabilities of each worst-case scenario happening and how permanent the effects are likely to be. Further information on Tim's technique for overcoming limiting factors can be found in Chapter 3 of "*The 4-Hour Work Week*".

Once you've written your worst-case scenarios and as many solutions as possible, you might end up with something like this:

Worst-Case Scenarios	Solutions
Running out of money in Outer Mongolia	• Have a separate bank account with £1000 emergency cash in it so that if you need to return home quickly you can. • Take a credit card with 0% interest on purchases with you so that if the worst happens you can buy a ticket to return home at any point and then start working again and pay off the card before any interest is charged.
Falling off the career ladder at home	• Mitigate this risk by taking a sabbatical rather than quitting. • Look into the possibility of freelance work you can do whilst away to ensure you're still gaining experience. • Check if there are activities or volunteer programmes that would be relevant to your current career that you can take part in when you feel like it on your travels. • Consider whether it actually matters. If your current career isn't the one you've always dreamed of, you could use this opportunity to pursue what you really want to do on returning.

This is your **Worst-Case Scenario List**.

If you really sit and give it some thought, I would put money on it that you'll be hard-pressed to find many worst-case scenarios that are insurmountable.

That is, unless you put things like death on the list, but let's face it, that could happen any time, anywhere. Sure there are some places in the world that are more dangerous than others, but if you're sensible and careful in your travels you're probably about as likely to get run over by a bus tomorrow as you are to die trekking up a mountain in Thailand.

This list may look daunting, but it is likely that as you get older you will have more commitments and the number of obstacles you have to overcome to travel will only accumulate. The list is never going to be shorter than it is right now. Also, the more able-bodied you are when travelling, the better.

Being older when you travel definitely has some benefits, so much so that Chapter 6 is dedicated to this topic, but travelling can involve a lot of sleeping in less than ideal conditions (sleeper buses, trains, boats, etc.) and physical exertion to get to some sights you may want to see.[6] The fewer physical restrictions you have, the easier your travels will be. And our physical constraints, just like our obstacles to being able to travel, are only likely to increase as we get older.

If you already have physical limitations or disabilities, you can of course find a way around these, and shouldn't let them stop you from travelling. However if you can avoid adding to whatever collection of ail-

---

[6] At 28 years old I struggled to make it up the 5,500 steps to get to the top of Adam's Peak in Sri Lanka.

ments you already have by not waiting another 10 years to travel, I'd highly recommend it.

Part 2

Overcoming the Obstacles

Chapter 3

Are You Sure It's an Obstacle?

"If you think you can or you think you can't, you're probably right."
Henry Ford

Unfortunately we live in a world where whenever we suggest an action that is off the beaten track, the accepted and anticipated response, from ourselves and friends, is to list the reasons why it's a bad idea. These objections then become the "reasons" not to do it.

We simply don't live in a society where our first response to something out of the ordinary is to smile and say, "Cool, that's different. Let me think of the reasons you should do that, or help come up with suggestions to overcome the obstacles stopping you."

We expect that if we try things that don't conform to the norm we will fail, an idea ingrained in our heads our whole lives. It's the expectation. Especially when it comes to things like people quitting their jobs to travel.

But just because people react with negativity and tell you your plan will fail, it doesn't mean you have to accept it.

"All my life people have said that I wasn't going to make it.... You can never quit. Winners never quit, and quitters never win."
Ted Turner

If you really want to do something, be that travel or anything else in life, *do it*. Decide to do it now, start working towards it, and ignore anyone who says you can't do it or will fail. Chances are the doubters are not living out their dreams and so want to put a downer on yours. If you read quotes by any successful entrepreneur, or people who have achieved great and different things from the norm, they all reinforce the idea that you can be and do whatever you want. If you believe it, you can do it.

You just need to get out of your own way. Stop seeing obstacles as problems. Focus on solutions and use those solutions to start seeing the "problems" as opportunities that can lead you to do great and better things.

"In the middle of difficulty lies opportunity."
Albert Einstein

You may have to work hard, but that means you will appreciate what you have achieved more when you get there. You have to push yourself, learn, and work out solutions to get what you really want.

There is an old Zen story that Ryan Holiday mentions in his book, *The Obstacle Is the Way*, which says:

"The obstacle in the path becomes the path. Never forget, within every obstacle is an opportunity to improve our condition."

I wanted to leave to travel a year earlier than I did, but I had another nine months left on my rental contract at that point, and there were other reasons that would have made it difficult to go right at that moment. But these didn't stop me from making the decision that I would go.

Once I made that decision, I could make the most out of that nine-month "obstacle". Instead of seeing it as a bad thing that stopped me from travelling, I turned it into an opportunity to better situate myself in my career and to save more money. In the end, it helped me travel for longer.

The nine months ended up being extremely beneficial, but only because I knew what I was working towards during that time. I'd made the decision I was going to travel, and I gained precious time in which to prepare and get myself into the best position to do so.

"A pessimist sees the difficulty in every opportunity; an optimist sees the opportunity in every difficulty."
Winston Churchill

Chapter 4

Money: You Don't Have to Be Rich to Travel Full-Time

"I feel that luck is preparation meeting opportunity."
Oprah Winfrey

"Don't worry about money, just make it work. Experience is far more valuable than money will ever be."
Anonymous

By far the most frequently cited obstacles to travel are a lack of money and pressing financial commitments, such as having a mortgage or other debts.

First, travelling does not cost as much as you would expect. You do not need to be rich to do it.

Let me repeat that one, it's important:

You do not need to be rich to travel.

A lot of people I meet say, "Oh, you're so lucky to be able to travel for so long; I wish I had enough money to do that."

The funny thing is, they probably already do, or at least could create a situation in which they would have enough money to travel very easily, and in a short amount of time.

But to do so you have to decide what's most important to you.

It's very easy when working to get sucked into a cycle of earning money to then spend on lots of things we don't actually need. We get wrapped up in what money can buy rather than the experiences money can facilitate. But, as a very wise Swedish proverb states:

"He who buys what he does not need steals from himself."

The first step to having enough money to travel is therefore changing your mind-set.

Make a conscious decision to place more emphasis and importance on experiences rather than material things and recognise that experiences create longer lasting happiness.[7]

---

[7] There have been numerous studies which show that whilst material possessions make us happy at first, over time our satisfaction with them goes down, whereas when it comes to experiences our happiness actually increases over time. Dr. Thomas Gilovich, Professor of Psychology at Cornell University, reported these findings following a number of studies on the subject of money and happiness.
(See www.news.cornell.edu/stories/2013/01/feel-happier-talk-about-experiences-not-things, accessed June 2016.)

This attitude is essential in helping you save money before you depart, and will also be an extremely beneficial mentality when actually travelling.

I'm not suggesting everyone should become monks and sell all their worldly possessions, but there may be *some* things you can sell in the build up to going away, and at the very least you can work towards not accumulating more.

When you travel you will be living out of one bag (for your own sanity I'd strongly suggest this be a backpack and not a wheelie bag). Anything that doesn't fit in that one bag will be left at home gathering dust whilst you're away.

It may have been nice and enjoyable as you progressed in your career to buy more expensive clothes or gadgets but you will not need these things when you travel, so *stop collecting them now.*

Halting this typical pattern of accumulating things will go a long way to helping you save money.

Also look for other ways you can cut down your expenses each month. Can you take packed lunches to work or find free activities to do on weekends?

If you usually take a short holiday each year, it's also worth considering staying at home this year instead. Yes, the break would probably be nice, but the amount of money most people spend on a week- or two-week-long holiday can probably pay for anywhere between a month and three months worth of travel elsewhere, depending on where you want to go. Remember, it's not as expensive as you think to travel. "Holidays" are usually expensive because the focus is on comfort and luxury to get the full amount of relaxation possible before returning to work. "Travel" on the other hand is usually more focused on adventure, and seeing a variety of locations or fully immersing yourself in the culture of one area. This difference means you naturally spend your time in different types of places, that are a lot more reasonably priced, than you would when on holiday.

The average person may spend £700 ($1000) on a week-long holiday in a nice relaxing resort in Spain but when travelling, rather than on holiday, that money would go *a lot* further. I lived off a lot less than £700 a month when I travelled in both Spain and France. And Europe is one of the more expensive places to travel.

I'm currently staying in Indonesia for a while and my fixed monthly expenses at this point in time consist of:

- Rent: £120
- Bills: £15
- Scooter Rental: £30
- Monthly Visa Extension: £17.50

Total £182.50 ($250)

That's less than £200 each month for my rent and transport (and I live in a *really* nice house). Sure, I still have to buy food and petrol for my scooter, but most meals cost about 50p to £2 (75¢ to $3) here, and a full tank of petrol is also only £1 ($1.50), so keeping daily expenses low is very easy.

In fact, I have a friend who just rented a place here for a year for £900 ($1250). For the *whole year*. That's roughly what my rent (including bills) used to cost me a *month* in London.

Money is not the obstacle to travelling. If you want to do it enough, you will find a way.

If you already live minimally and saving genuinely isn't an option for you, travel is still possible. There are volunteering programmes that will help subside costs by providing food and accommodation, or options to work in different countries, whether in a bar or as an English teacher.

If you want it, you will find a way, but the first thing to change has to be your mind-set. Shift yourself to focus on how much more valuable experiences are than possessions, and think of money as the thing that will enable those experiences.

Financial commitments, such as mortgages or other debts, may also be at the crux of what has prevented you from travelling until now.

I have met so many people who say, "I'd love to travel but I have a mortgage." On the contrary, having a property has been extremely helpful in allowing me to travel for an extended period of time.

For most people, renting out your property to others whilst travelling will not only cover your mortgage but will also leave you with some profit each month.[8] Even if it's only a small amount of profit, every little

---

[8] You will need to convert your mortgage into a buy-to-let mortgage or get a temporary consent-to-let from your mortgage provider to do this. For more advice on renting out properties and types of mortgages, visit www.ThePropertyBuyingExperts.com, which is a free property advice service. I am a co-founder of this website but I do not make any money by your visiting the site and all advice is free. This suggestion is made purely to help those who feel trapped by their mortgage and need a little extra advice working out how they can use their property to enable their travels.

bit extra really does help. If you make £50 profit a month, that could buy you somewhere between 25 and 100 meals where I am at the moment!

If you have other debts, I'd strongly suggest trying to clear these before you go. If that just isn't feasible, however, you can get an interest-free balance transfer credit card. As long as your travels aren't more than two years (the maximum interest free period that is usually available), and you make the minimum payment each month, this will take the pressure off repaying the full debt till you're back earning money again.[9]

---

[9] If you're from the UK, www.MoneySavingExpert.com is the best place to compare different options of interest-free balance transfer credit cards.

Chapter 5

Work: You're Not Going to Miss Anything

"How much I missed, simply because I was afraid of missing it."
Paulo Coelho

"'I wish I had never gone travelling.' Said no one. Ever."
Anonymous

I have always been extremely ambitious, so the thought that taking time off would put me behind in my career progression played on my mind a lot before I started to travel.

But you know what? As soon as you step out of that cycle where work consumes most of your life, it no longer seems to matter so much.

Once you appreciate what it's like to not have the constant background stress of work and other commitments, you start enjoying life so much more that being behind in your career seems like the most insignificant worry in the world. It feels absurd that you could potentially have let it stop you from gaining such a beneficial life experience.

And travel is just that. A hugely beneficial life experience, both for you personally and in terms of your career development.

What you learn whilst travelling may actually put you ahead of those who have spent that same time working. You will grow in actual skills and qualifications, and become a far more interesting person, making others more eager to hire and work with you. That's because travelling teaches you things about life, about yourself, about how to be patient, how to be kind, how to be accepting. And most importantly it reawakens your mind.

Once you've travelled you may even find you don't want to go back to the industry you were in before. Either way, travelling will in some way make you better at whatever you did before and at the very least make you a much more appealing person to interview.

People want to hire people they like, not robots. When you apply for any job, the person doing the hiring will probably have piles of CVs to sift through. If you have developed some intriguing and different hobbies and qualifications whilst travelling, you will catch more attention than the person who lists their interests as reading and watching movies.

For example, from my years of travelling I can now list these interests, achievements, and skills:

- **Languages**: Spanish – advanced, French – intermediate, Indonesian – intermediate.
- **Qualifications and achievements**: Author of *What Clients Really Want (And The S**t That*

Drives Them Crazy) and *Travel for Your Life*. Certified yoga teacher. Open water and advanced scuba diver. Website Developer (HTML, CSS, and JavaScript).

- **Hobbies**: Surfing, Salsa, Writing.

Now most of these are not related to what was, and may well be again, my chosen career in marketing and advertising. I think it's unlikely that most advertising agencies or companies looking for marketing consultants will care that I speak Indonesian or that I'm a certified yoga teacher, but it will certainly make my CV more interesting. It proves that I'm keen on learning and exploring different things. It says something about my personality, and that has a huge effect on how well a person will do at a particular job.

There may even be things you end up doing or learning while travelling that help your career in a way you never expected.

One of the items on my list above is a book called *What Clients Really Want (And The S**t That Drives Them Crazy)*, which is aimed at advertising agencies and directly related to my previous career. I never intended to write a book on advertising when I left to travel, but one of the most beautiful things about travelling is that it gives you time. It gives you head space to think and the freedom to do whatever you want to do. For me it turned out that what I really wanted to do was write.

I didn't have to do it. It was never a chore or work. I just wanted to.

I haven't re-entered the world of marketing and advertising yet, but I have no doubt if I do that having written a book on the subject will be more beneficial to my career than having spent another year slaving away working 70-hour weeks.

I'm not saying you should write a book; that may not be what you want to do. But removing stress from your life and having time to try new things will open up new possibilities of what you can do.

When I was working full time, whenever I read a book or watched something it was with the sole purpose of entertainment and relaxation. But I don't need to do that anymore since I don't have any stress to recover from.[10] So I started reading books and listening to podcasts about a huge range of topics that would teach me about subjects I'm interested in. I finally had the mental space to do that. And some of those books have been on marketing and advertising, which means I have actually learnt more about the field I work in, and will have a more varied and broad set of things to talk about in any job interview when I return.

Even if you don't increase your skills in your chosen field or discover something completely different that you love, you will at least make your CV more interesting with the new things you discover. You will also learn some hugely important life skills as you travel that could apply to any job.

For example, you'll learn how to:
- be more flexible
- negotiate well
- be tolerant of others

---

[10] Of course there are some stresses when travelling but they are of a very different nature to working life and generally tend to be much more transient.

- be resourceful
- fend for yourself
- be calm under pressure
- distinguish important from unimportant details
- ask for help
- be creative

The importance of this last point, *be creative*, should not be underestimated. You may not work in a creative industry but new ideas about how to do things, or new thinking patterns related to products or services, are beneficial in any job and role. Travel will open and wake up your mind again and allow these to come in.

"Innovative thinkers are constantly asking the question, how can we make things better? No matter what stage you're at in your career or what industry you work in, everyone around you can benefit from new ideas. Don't be afraid to think outside the box—just because something works doesn't mean it can't be better."
Brett Wilson

Travel gives you this because:

"For good ideas and innovation, you need human interaction, conflict, argument, debate."
Margaret Heffernan

Every day you travel you will get these things in abundance, because you will see and meet new and fascinating people every single day. Meeting such a large variety of people daily can't fail to cause you to look at and think about the world in different ways. Even any conflicts that arise will help expand your thinking by forcing you to think of potential solutions to the situation, and conflict resolution is useful skill in any industry.

Travel will not hinder your career. If anything, it might be just the thing you need to reignite it.

Chapter 6

Age: You Are Not Too Old

The majority of people seem to think that if they didn't take a gap year to travel before or after university, it's too late. They've "missed their chance" and are now resigned to wishing they'd travelled when they were younger.

There is absolutely no reason this need be the case. Yes, you have more commitments as you get older, but as we've already seen, they are just things we need to work around and can even be beneficial in some instances, such as gaining rental income from a house you own.

It can, in fact, also be a lot more enjoyable to travel when you're older.

If you've worked for a number of years first, and especially if you've had a stressful job, you will appreciate so much more the time and freedom that travelling gives you. When you've just finished school, you're still used to having long breaks throughout the year to simply be you and enjoy yourself. Once you start working, however, the longest break you're likely to get is two weeks, and more often than not you'll be so exhausted or stressed from work that it will take you the first week to relax. Then before you know it, you're back to work. You now understand how important that time off is, but have hardly any of it.

Just think how free you would feel if instead of two weeks you had six months, or even a year?

A lot of travellers just out of school or university, especially if they are on the road for a long time, also partly rely on "the Bank of Mum and Dad". When you travel when you're older, you will no doubt be the one paying and it is much better that way. If you've had to work hard, making sacrifices along the way, and really dedicate your time and energy to be able to travel, your appreciation of the experience will dramatically increase.

As we get older, most people also get better at handling the little challenges life throws at us. We learn to deal with mishaps more effectively, become more practical, and realise we can actually handle most situations—all essential skills when travelling.

For example, when I was in Sri Lanka in 2015, I missed my train stop at one point. I'd only been in Sri Lanka a handful of days, was in the third-class carriage, the only woman, didn't speak the language, and it was night time. I asked the people in my carriage what I should do (thankfully a couple of them spoke some broken English). They said I needed to stay on another three stops to get to the next big town so I could get a tuk-tuk[11] back from there.

---

[11] A tuk-tuk is a taxi that's constructed out of a motorbike and carriage attached to the back providing space for passengers. In a lot of Southeast Asia this is the most common and cheapest form of transport, although the name for these three-wheeled taxis varies from tuk-tuk to auto to auto-rickshaw depending on the country you're in.

Obviously I wasn't happy that I'd made the mistake, and especially not when I realised I couldn't just get off at the next stop and go ten minutes back to my destination, but instead would have to travel forty minutes in the wrong direction and *then* go back again.

If that had happened to me when I was 18 or 21, I probably would have cried at that moment. It was dark, I was tired, and I dreaded to think how much a tuk-tuk ride back would cost me.[12]

Instead, as a 28-year-old, I realised that neither the money nor the fact I'd missed my stop mattered. There was nothing I could do to change the situation by that point. If I have to spend £10 ($15) to get myself out of a bad situation, I will. In fact I'll actually be happy that I'm able to resolve the problem rather than breaking down. As long as I physically have access to the money, it doesn't matter. The £10 will come back one day and if it makes my trip half a day shorter as a result, so be it. There's no point crying over it. It has already happened and isn't going to change.

As they say in the serenity prayer:

"Give me the serenity to accept the things I cannot change, courage to change the things I can, and wisdom to know the difference."

---

[12] In fact I can almost guarantee I would have cried in that same situation when younger. When I first arrived in France at the age of 21, I burst into tears on a tram when I was fined for not having a ticket, even though all that happened was I lost some money and it was my fault for not buying one in the first place. Not one of my finest moments.

Or as my dad always told me when growing up, if anything bad happened:

"Laugh or cry, it won't change the situation so you might as well laugh, at least it will make you feel better about it."

As well as becoming better able to handle difficult situations, as we get older our outlook also changes.

There's liberation in knowing you're no longer so naïve and are more sure of yourself. More certain of what you do and don't like doing, less concerned about what others think, and more open to trying new things.

I find myself saying yes to suggestions, even when they're silly, far more frequently now than I would have done when I was younger. Especially if someone suggests something I've never done before, as then I think, "I can't believe I got to this age without having done that, why the hell not." Or to put it another way:

"Young enough to know I can, old enough to know I shouldn't, stupid enough to do it anyway."
Anonymous

Chapter 7

The Joys of Going Solo

If you've got no one to travel with, that's great.

I genuinely couldn't be happier for you.

Having no one to go with is possibly the best thing that could happen to you when deciding to go travelling. If you want to have the most interesting, varied, and truly organic experience, travelling solo is the way to do it.

Lots of people go travelling with friends, lovers, or relatives and enjoy it. But travelling with another person can be tough and more often than not those who start travelling together end by splitting up at some point along the way and sometimes ruin their relationships forever in the process.

The reason it's so difficult to travel with someone else is because travel is such a personal thing and there are so many options as to what you can do each day. Unless you and your travel buddy have practically identical interests and personalities, there are likely to be disagreements and arguments at some point.

Remember also that there will be lots of early mornings when travelling, journeys to be taken when one or both of you are cranky and tired, and there will be things that go wrong that one of you inevitably blames the other for.

People can vary in their ideas of what good travel consists of and what they want to achieve during their time abroad. Unless you match up perfectly with your travel buddy, it is likely to cause disagreement at some point.

Travelling with others will also stop you from making as many new friends. When travelling with a companion there is simply not the same need to socialise as much, so you naturally make less effort to meet new people.

Usually I meet new people pretty much every day but when I met up with two friends from home while travelling for a couple of weeks, I didn't meet anyone else that entire time. We had no need to talk to others. We had the occasional conversation with a stranger but didn't make any friends. That was fine with me at the time, as it was just a two-week interlude in my longer journey which does involve meeting new people all the time; but if the whole of my trip was like that, the experiences I've had so far wouldn't have been nearly as rich or stimulating.

On my travels I have met some of the most genuinely fascinating people with whom I have huge amounts in common...which is hardly surprising as we're all partaking in the same activity. Clearly we all share some underlying character trait causing us to travel. In fact without some of the people I met on my travels I would never have had the courage to write my first book, let alone this one. And I can guarantee I wouldn't have met most of those people if I had the safety net of travelling with a companion.

Meeting People

A common worry that comes at the thought of travelling alone is, *"But I don't want to be on my own the whole time. I'll get lonely. How am I going to meet people?"*

Most of the time this question answers itself.

If you stay in hostels where there are common areas, a lot of the time you would be genuinely hard-pushed *not* to meet people if you tried. In fact, I have sat in a common room, exhausted, not wanting to talk to anyone, only to have at least three people come up to have a chat even though I looked engrossed in what I was doing and had my headphones in.

Meeting people is *incredibly* easy most of the time.

The reason is, if you're travelling and staying in hostels, there will be a lot of other people in the same boat, who are travelling alone and want to meet people, too.

When travelling, it is not seen as at all odd to be on your own, and people strike up conversations with strangers all the time, especially in the safety of hostels where they know most people will be receptive to a new person talking to them.

Since everyone is much more friendly and open than normal, the depth of the friendships you can make in only a 24-hour period will amaze you.

Of course there will be times when it's harder to meet others. That means, if you're travelling on your own and want some company, you'll have to make an effort to ensure that happens. But this doesn't usually require anything more than simply saying "hi" to a few people.

For the Shy Ones

For those who are really confident, the "just go talk to people in your hostel" advice is a lot easier, I know. For extroverts, as long as there are people around, they will meet others easily without any difficulties.

For people who are shy, however, this can be a source of worry. I have met countless others who worried about this before leaving for their travels. Myself included.

About a year before I went away, due to an unfortunate series of events in my personal life, I'd ended up so insecure and lacking in confidence that I would start to sweat just if someone asked me how I was. Talking to people made me *that* nervous.

I spent time working on trying to be more confident again before I departed, but aspects of this lack of confidence were very much still with me when I left.

I found, though, that the longer I travelled on my own the more my confidence came back to me. And that's mostly because it *had to*.

I had to learn to talk to random people again and remember that there is nothing to be scared of. What's the worst that can happen? The person might say they're busy and can't talk right now. That's fine, move onto the next person. If you're looking for an ice breaker, ask where someone is from. It's not too personal but starts a conversation and gives you enough information from which to talk about other things.

Use travel as a way to work on the things that you wish you were better at or that you know are personal weaknesses. If shyness and a lack of confidence are some of your weaknesses, definitely travel on your own.

It's easier to be confident in new situations, because the stakes are low. Who cares if the people you meet don't like you, you'll never see them again if they don't.

Use travel as an opportunity to grow.

When It's Hard

There are some places where it will be harder to meet people.

For example, in some countries that are less touristy there are no hostels, so you have to stay in hotel rooms alone, removing one of the best places for meeting others.

In other places it might be that the hostel you're staying in just isn't very well set up for meeting people easily, with no common room or spaces where people can spend time together.[13]

I've found myself in such situations a number of times. Occasionally I like to be on my own so if one of these situations occurs when I'm feeling like some alone time anyway, I just embrace it and do my own thing.

Yes, that does mean you will probably end up having dinner by yourself at some point or even a beer, but so what? Take a good book with you or people-

---

[13] Although dorms are shared spaces, it's rare for people to spend long amounts of time hanging out in them as they're generally cramped, a little too warm, and there is almost always at least one person sleeping no matter what time of day it is.

watch and enjoy the solitude. I can promise you no one is judging you except for yourself.

If you find yourself in one of these situations but do want company then you've got to go out and find it. Book yourself on a tour that other backpackers are likely to go on, go to the local restaurant most highly recommended in *Lonely Planet* in that location,[14] or find something like a pool party going on during the day where people will be more open and friendly than in a bar at night. You'll be surprised how easy it is to meet people if you get out there and do something.

And if it doesn't work, that's okay too. Have some alone time in that place and know that you will meet people in the next place you go.

---

[14] For those who aren't familiar with the *Lonely Planet*, it is the largest travel guide publisher in the world. They produce guide books both on specific countries and continents. The information contained in these books is incredibly detailed with maps, accommodation listings, restaurants, and recommended activities, among other things. A large number of travellers take these guides with them on their trips or access the information from *Lonely Planet* online, meaning that the most highly recommended restaurant in the *Lonely Planet* is likely to be filled with other backpackers. I have seen entire streets lined with empty restaurants, but with one seemingly identical restaurant overflowing with people. It's always the one in the *Lonely Planet*. Tripadvisor.com is also becoming more popular as a reference for how to find the best and most popular backpacker restaurants in any area.

Part 3

What You'll Gain

Chapter 8

The Return of Your Life

"Normal is getting dressed in clothes you buy for work and driving through traffic in a car that you are still paying for—in order to get to a job you need to pay for the clothes and the car, and the house you leave vacant all day so you can afford to live in it."
Ellen Goodman

"So many people spend their health gaining wealth, and then have to spend their wealth to regain their health."
A.J. Reb Materi

I read a blog post not long ago from a guy in his late twenties who has been travelling for a number of years which talked about how he faces this constant dilemma between wanting to travel more and feeling like he should go home and start his real life. You know, settle down, get a sensible job with good career progression, and buy a house.

I found it so incredibly sad to read.

Why should it be assumed that what he's doing right now is any less valuable than if he were working in a sensible job saving up to one day buy a house and settle down with a couple of children?

Just because it's not what most people do doesn't make it any less worthwhile. In fact it's reported that 70% of people aren't happy with their jobs.[15] As long as the author of that blog is doing what makes him happy, he's doing the most important thing he possibly could do at this moment.

There is no point in having a job and a house just for the sake of it, but most people have a job purely because they need to pay the bills.

As the quote by Ellen Goodman very accurately points out, most of the bills we have are only there in the first place because we need certain things in order to be able to do that job. That is, a house close to the job, appropriate clothes, etc.

Over the previous seven years of working almost all of the clothes I bought were those appropriate for work, clothes that made me look smart enough and would portray the right image. As I started earning more money, the more expensive the clothes I bought for that job.

I earned money and then would instantly spend it on rent, commuting to and from my job, and on clothes for that job. Sure, I would spend some of it on going out with friends and enjoying myself, but most of the time I was too exhausted to really do anything after work. The main thing my friends and I did

---

[15] State of the American Workplace study conducted by Gallup in 2013 in which 70% of participants described themselves as "disengaged" from their work.
(www.gallup.com/services/178514/state-american-workplace.aspx, accessed June, 2016.)

was to go for drinks in order to get over the stress of work.

I wasn't gaining anything tangible or particularly enjoyable from all that money I earned every month, just the means to support my current lifestyle. It was a lifestyle that had me spending over a third of each week behind a desk, another third of it asleep, and the other third doing whatever I could to get over the stress of the first third.

If that's normal, I'm not so sure I want it.

As Elizabeth Gilbert points out in *Eat Pray Love*:

"We all inevitably work too hard, then we get burned out and have to spend the weekend in our pyjamas, eating cereal straight out of the box and staring at the TV in a mild coma (which is the opposite of working, yes, but not exactly the same thing as pleasure)."

Do you want to spend your whole life waiting for the weekend, or do you want your life to *be* the weekend?

If you take out the expenses you have to fulfil your job, the expenses we really truly have are very few. We need food, some clothing. and a roof over our heads. Aside from that, as humans we don't need much more. And those basic things we need to live cost a lot less in some countries than others.

The saddest thing about doing a job to pay for the things we need for that job is that most people aren't doing a job they love, just one which pays the bills.

The guy whose blog I read, debating whether to rejoin normal life, may during his travels discover the very thing at which he excels or loves but wasn't aware of previously. At least that means if he does choose to go home at some point and work, or even work abroad, he has a much better chance of landing a job in something he actually wants to do. It could be that he discovers that he loves teaching and helping people, so begins setting up schools to teach under-privileged children. Or it may be that he discovers he really loves travelling and so wants to tell other people about it to inspire them, too.

Think about the people who set up the Lonely Planet company. They decided to pursue their dreams, which for them consisted of travelling across Europe and Asia overland all the way to Australia. They didn't focus on earning lots of money. They instead focused on doing what they believed would make them happiest. And when they finished their travels, they started to write travel books, now with over 120 million copies in print in 11 languages.

If we remove the stress and expense of our jobs, there is less pressure to find a job just because it pays well. Instead you can focus on what you really enjoy doing first. Maybe one day you can turn it into something that will make you enough money to live. It's only without such extreme financial pressure that we are truly able to know that the work we're doing is what we genuinely want to do and love, not just what we have to do to survive.

Take your life back. Focus on what you actually want to do, not what you feel you should do.

"Believe that things will work out… follow your intuition and curiosity … trust your heart even when it leads you off the well-worn path.… You have to trust that the dots will somehow connect in your future.… The only way to do great work is to love what you do. If you haven't found it yet, keep looking.

Don't settle. As with all matters of your heart you'll know when you find it.... Have the courage to follow your heart and intuition. They somehow already know what you want to become, everything else is secondary."

Steve Jobs

Chapter 9

Being a Child Again

"Years may wrinkle the skin, but to give up enthusiasm wrinkles the soul."
Samuel Ullman

I now wake up every morning and can't wait to get out of bed and start my day.

You're allowed to hate me for saying that. I would have hated me for saying that before, since I have always been someone who woke up grumpy no matter how much sleep I'd had or whether it was the weekend or a weekday. I never wanted to get out of bed and I'd certainly never wake up thinking "Let's go!"

But that has completely changed now. Because I'm travelling for a long time and on my own, I can do whatever I want at any point. It's completely my decision. So when I wake up each day I'm excited because I know I'm going to go do just that, rather than what I think I should, or what I need to do out of obligation.

Even if I go for a night out and got to bed late, waking up tired and a bit groggy from too much beer,

I still start the day with an overwhelming feeling of joyful anticipation.

It's not the "Let's go" I used to experience when working, where I would wake up on weekends and feel the need to get out of bed so as not to waste my weekend doing silly things like "relaxing". It's not a time-pressured fear of missing out. It's childish excitement making me want to run out of my room and get on with life.

In *Neither Here nor There*, Bill Bryson explains some of the ways travelling makes you like a child, writing:

"Suddenly you are five years old again. You can't read anything, you only have the most rudimentary sense of how things work, you can't even reliably cross the street without endangering your life. Your whole existence becomes a series of interesting guesses."

I love this quote, but this is not all of it. Travelling also makes us like children again in a much more profound way. It reminds us of the excitement of life.

Remember when you were a child and used to wake up early, running into your parents' room wanting to go play, explore, and generally just mess around? Or how exciting and mesmerising the simplest of things could be? How you used to be interested in different sports and activities and have the energy to do them?

That's what travel gives you back.

I took part in so many sports, activities, and hobbies as a child, just for fun. As I got older, however, the number of things I would do just for the enjoyment of them severely dropped off. I only did the things I had to.

51

My interest in other activities started to decrease as I went through university but really took a nosedive when I started working, especially as I got busier and more stressed over the years. Anything other than working, and relaxing to get over the stress of working, basically fell off the radar.

What travel gives you back is *time* and *options*.

If you decide to travel for any length of time, you have essentially decided that you can do whatever the hell you want in that time.

When I left to go travelling my dad said to me, "But aren't you going to get bored? What are you going to do every day?"

I didn't know the answer to that, I still don't from one day to the next, but I definitely don't expect to be bored at any point. If I get bored for any sustained period of time, I have to conclude that I myself am the problem, since I have given myself a free pass to do whatever it is that takes my fancy.

A lot of the things we enjoy may very well have been forgotten over the years of not having any time, or only being able to do them when tired, which makes them feel like a chore. Once you start travelling, though, you have time again. When you were a kid, you went to school but there were a lot of hours outside of that and on weekends where the only thing you had to worry about was how to fill your time with fun.

This is what you do when you travel, *fill your time with fun*.

What that fun consists of will depend completely on you.

The longer you travel the more activities you will remember or discover that you think are fun. It might be that you discover that you think temples are the most fascinating thing in the world and want to see as many as possible; or it could be that you learn you love a new sport and want to do it as much as you can, just in the same way that a child begs their parents to let them go out and ride their bike; they just can't get enough of it.

Obviously if your trip is only a few weeks long it will be harder to rediscover these things, since the amount of fun you can explore and try will be time limited.

When on a shorter trip it's also likely that most of your activities will be focused on the types of things you enjoy doing and seeing when in a new place, but you absolutely can still rediscover the things you love in that time, if you explore everything with the wide-eyed enthusiasm of a child.

There may be some things you realise you don't enjoy too. For example, I find museums incredibly dull. But when you find the things you do like and approach them with the childish enthusiasm that gets beaten out of us as we're made to grow up and do sensible adult things, you'll start to remember how pleasurable life can be.

Chapter 10

Waking Up Your Brain

"Most people die at 25 and aren't buried until they're 75."
Benjamin Franklin

I never realised until I quit my job and started travelling that somewhere over the years of working I'd stopped thinking and started sleepwalking my way through life.

I used to think about all sorts of things. I studied philosophy at university because I enjoy thinking and asking questions, but somewhere in the spiral of being constantly busy trying to fit everything in and "enjoy my life" whilst having a really busy job, I stopped thinking and forgot the curiosity and love of learning that had been part of who I am.

I cannot even begin to describe how good it felt as my brain started going again as I travelled; to have thoughts and questions swimming around, to be excited about learning and doing new things.

I never thought I'd be someone who would write a book, I'd never understood the desire to … but when my thoughts started bubbling up again there were so many of them that I almost *had* to.

Travelling gave me the time and space to stop and think enough to actually have something to say. To have an opinion and the time to explore it with something I found enjoyable, writing.

For you it may not be writing, but if you want to find out what you might be interested in, you've got to give your brain time and space. You need to stop making your brain so busy with all the things you've got to do in a day and instead allow it the time to wonder.

You'll be amazed at what you discover.

There's a great article by Heidi Hackemer describing how she'd been unhappy at work but unable to figure out what other things she might like to do. After having quit her job to travel, she realised the reason she hadn't had that flash of inspiration before was because:

"I never sat still long enough for the lightning bolt to find me.
A bored mind is a receptive mind.
A bored mind is a self-aware mind.
A bored mind is a creative mind.
I was never bored.
I was filled to the brim with distraction and busyness. Chock
full of doing.
My company needed me.
My twitter account needed me.
My emails needed me.
Actually, that's all shit.
My soul needed me.
But I wasn't tending to it at all."

Give yourself the space to find out what it is that makes you tick. What makes you feel alive and causes your brain to buzz with a thousand thoughts.

Chapter 11

Enjoying Life More

"Nobody can give you freedom. Nobody can give you equality or justice or anything. If you're a man, you take it."
Malcolm X

In quitting your job to travel, you give yourself time to do whatever you want during your day. Which means that for the first time in years, possibly ever, you are now totally free.

You have given yourself the gift of freedom.

You can do whatever you want to do *every day*. So enjoy the moment, take things slow, and enjoy the freedom you have to suddenly decide to do something new one day, or move on to a new place, or sit around and do nothing. This is one of the most important things you gain in travelling.

When working we spend our whole lives rushing from one thing to the next and therefore our brain is always onto the next thing on our to-do list rather than on the thing we're doing at that moment in time.

When taking a bus back home I'd never just enjoy the journey; I'd be thinking about what I had to do at the other end. When going to the gym I'd be thinking about what I needed to get done at work afterwards. Even when meeting up with friends I wouldn't be fully in the moment, I'd be thinking about what time I'd have to leave to get to the next thing in my busy day, or the like.

When doing anything, as soon as you start thinking about the next thing you are no longer fully enjoying and engaging in the current activity. You are not enjoying the actual moment you're in.

In one of my favourite books, *Zen and the Art of Motorcycle Maintenance*, Robert M. Pirsig explains this sentiment perfectly, saying:

> *"I don't want to hurry it…. When you want to hurry something, that means you no longer care about it and want to get onto other things."*

Think about the last time you did something when you were fully and only engaged in that activity at that moment in time. I would have struggled to find an example of something before I went travelling.

That's because we usually have so much to do and so little time, that we rush around trying to cram it all in rather than taking enjoyment in one thing.

As David Cain, founder of Raptitude.com, put it after coming back from travelling and returning to the working world:

> *"Suddenly I have a lot more money and a lot less time…. While I was abroad I wouldn't have thought twice about spending the day wandering through a national park or reading my*

book on the beach for a few hours. Now that kind of stuff feels like it's out of the question. Doing either one would take most of one of my precious weekend days!"

Use the freedom you've given yourself to really enjoy each thing you do rather than always thinking about the next.

You'll find that if you start to actually pay attention to what you're doing, keeping your awareness in each current moment rather than the future, everything you do and see will become so much more interesting than you ever realised before.

"When reading, only read. When eating, only eat. When thinking, only think."
Seung Sahn

I have learnt to appreciate so many things more since doing this: sitting still, watching birds fly in the sky, looking at clouds, walking (anywhere and everywhere), looking at a view, food. The list goes on.

A lot of these surprise me. I have spent most of my adult years pressed for time, so the idea of sitting and just enjoying the view or watching clouds, was absurd to me. Why would anyone waste all that time? You could be doing something. Getting something done.

I always had somewhere to be or something to do.

One of my favourite activities in the world now is sitting and watching clouds. Clouds are amazing. They're so incredibly beautiful. Yet I never saw them before, because I never bothered to look. But now I look. I seek them out.

"If you change the way you look at things, the things you look at change."
Wayne Dyer

There are so many small things that I now find so incredibly beautiful because I pay attention; it makes each day so much more enjoyable than it otherwise would have been.

I know that sounds pretentious but it's the truth. Once you slow down and pay attention to what you're doing in each moment rather than always looking to the future, you will see it too. As I've become more present in the moment, my perception has actually changed. I now see things as more beautiful than I ever have before in my life.

Travel gives you the time and freedom to do this so you can enjoy and appreciate every part of your life more.

Chapter 12

This Is F***ing Awesome

At least once every day I find myself thinking how my life is pretty good now.

Yes, there are still bad bits sometimes and my life isn't just a bed of roses but overall the majority of it is pretty good and there is at least one moment every day where I think this, whatever this is at that moment, is pretty f***ing awesome.

I don't say that to make you jealous. I say it to help make sure you really, really know why it pays off to take the risk (and it's not even really a risk) and travel.

My life hasn't always been like this. I used to work 70-hour weeks; I was so stressed that I'd cry at work at least once a week, and was on the verge of a nervous breakdown.

However, having gone through that makes this experience all the better. I value it so much more. I appreciate how great my life is on a daily basis in comparison to what it could have been had I not decided to change things and go travelling.

If you feel in any way dissatisfied with your life currently and think, "I wish I could travel", just go do it.

You have everything to gain.

"For the past 33 years, I have looked in the mirror every morning and asked myself: 'If today were the last day of my life, would I want to do what I am about to do today?' And whenever the answer has been 'No' for too many days in a row, I know I need to change something.... Almost everything—almost all external expectations, all pride, all fear of embarrassment or failure—these things just fall away in the face of death, leaving only what is truly important. Remembering that you are going to die is the best way I know to avoid the trap of thinking you have something to lose."

Steve Jobs

Part 4

Safety

Chapter 13

"But It's Scary Out There"

"Do one thing every day that scares you."
Eleanor Roosevelt

"99% of things we worry about never happen."
Anonymous

"The fear of the event is often worse than the event itself."
Anonymous

Don't avoid travelling because you're scared.

The more you travel the more you will realise how similar everywhere in the world really is.

And I don't mean in a boring "it's all the same" way.

What I mean is that in most places the fundamentals aren't actually that different and people are nice and friendly. Yes, there are bad people out there who will try to steal things, and so on, but that's the same in every country, including the one you call home.

Obviously certain countries have higher risks of this than others, but as long as you are careful and sensible the risks of something bad happening are greatly reduced.[16]

I have been travelling for almost two years now on my own, across nine countries and so far the worst things that have happened to me are: an airline lost my luggage (but later returned it), I've had food poisoning (once), and have been locked out of the hotel I was staying in for 30 minutes at 2:00 a.m. (no one accosted or tried to mug me in that time, though).[17]

All three of those things could quite easily have happened to me living in England and just taking a weekend trip abroad.

---

[16] It is worth noting that there are of course some areas of the world which are very dangerous because they are currently war zones or there is a lot of terrorist activity. By all means, if you do your research and find there are still places that are safe to go within those areas, go. I personally prefer to just avoid those areas for now. There will hopefully be a time in the future when those places are safe again and the world's a big place, so I'll continue exploring other parts until then.

[17] I have also had human sewage accidentally flicked up the back of my legs whilst having open gaping wounds on both of my heels. That's probably the worst thing that's happened to me so far but that's quite specific, so I think you're unlikely to fall foul to the same fate.

You Don't Need to Be Brave to Travel

I met an older lady who works on a beach where I was travelling a while ago and who goes by the name of Mama Loco. She's a larger than life lady who will remind you of your grandma and is full of joy and humour, but also a little bit crazy (hence the name).

When talking to her, I mentioned that I'm travelling alone. She looked shocked and said, "You must have great power; you are very brave."

I am not brave.

It's not brave to travel on your own as a guy or a girl.

As well as most of the world being much more similar than you would expect, what I've also discovered in travelling is that the majority of people are welcoming, kind and have good intentions. Just as if you saw a foreigner who needed help back home you would volunteer your assistance, so do the majority of people in other countries. Of course, you need to be wary and make sure you don't just blindly trust people, but most of the time people aren't out to get you.

I shared this thought with Mama Loco, who replied, "Well, you are friendly, so people will be to you, too. A smile will get you a long way."

And she's right. If you're friendly and nice to people, they're much more likely to act that way towards you in return. If you're stand offish and rude to others, the chances of them being nice to you are very slim.

> *"If you give a punch, you'll get a punch.*
> *If you give a smile, you'll get a smile."*
> **Anonymous**

I have heard wonderful stories of people being helped out by others when bad things have happened on their travels.

For example, I had some friends whose hotel room was broken into when in India. The owners of the hotel were so horrified at the theft that they told the whole village about it so if anyone was seen trying to sell my friends' belongings, they would know. Within a week all of their possessions were returned to them.

Even with smaller things, most people I've met on my travels have shown honesty and kindness.

I lost a necklace at a market one day in Myanmar (the chain had broken and the pendant fell off), so a friend and I started looking around on the floor for it.

One of the shopkeepers stopped my friend to ask what we were looking for, so he explained and described the necklace, which it turned out the shopkeeper had found.

The shopkeeper who found it sold jewellery and could quite easily have kept the pendant to sell and make some money from rather than volunteering the information that she'd found it and returning it. I tried to give the woman some money to say thank you, but she wouldn't accept it. She hadn't found and reunited me with the necklace for any personal gain, just because it was the right thing to do.

Bad things or unexpected scenarios may happen from time to time, but as long as you're still alive and safe whatever it is really isn't that bad.

"The man who is truly good and wise will bear with dignity whatever fortune sends, and will always make the best of his circumstances."
Aristotle

Chapter 14

Tips for Staying Safe

Even though most people are friendly and well meaning, it is definitely worthwhile to actively take steps to lessen the risk of anything undesirable happening on your travels.

Here are the behaviours I have found to be most beneficial in preventing unwanted situations from happening to you whilst travelling.

1. When you can, avoid arriving places after dark and exploring cities and towns for the first time when it's dark. There will be some instances in which it's unavoidable, however the fewer times you do it, the less risk.

2. If you have to arrive somewhere really late at night or early morning, ask the hostel where you're staying if they can arrange a taxi or tuk-tuk with someone they trust to collect you. Sometimes this might cost a pound or two more, but it is much better to spend that extra money than potentially take a journey in an

unlicensed vehicle in a city you don't know with all your belongings on you in the dark.

3. If you will be arriving at night, book your first night's accommodation in advance. I have met lots of travellers who don't book accommodation in advance and this is definitely less of an issue if travelling in a group, but if you're on your own, do you really want to be wandering around the streets at night looking for somewhere to stay with everything you own on you? I wouldn't even want to do that at home.

4. If you're not going to book one night's accommodation in advance, research the areas in that town or city at least a little bit first, so that you know you aren't just wondering around the dodgy part of town with all your possessions.

5. Always insist on a locker in your accommodation for at least your passport, and if that isn't a possibility, hide it somewhere in your room, such as in your pillowcase, under the sheet of a made bed, so if someone breaks in and just grabs your bags, your passport won't be ready and waiting for them in one place.[18]

---

[18] When travelling your passport is by far your most valuable possession, followed by a working ATM card. If you have those two things even if all your possessions were stolen you'd still be able to get by. Even if you have just your passport you'd still be able to get by, since you'd at least be able to prove who you are for someone to transfer some money to you until the lost or stolen items are replaced.

6. Don't take valuables of any description out. I've heard of so many stories of people who've lost their passports or expensive phones whilst out as they've been pickpocketed. Unfortunately this does happen, but you don't need those things on you when you're out, so don't take them.

7. Never walk with your phone out in your hand in front of you—so much phone theft happens like this in England even and it's no different when travelling.

8. Don't put your wallet or anything valuable in your back pocket.

9. Always check if the place you're staying has a time at which they close their doors and if they do, what the procedure is for getting in after that time. A surprisingly large number of places I've stayed lock up at a certain time. At one point I stood at the end of the road to my hotel banging on a 10-foot metal gate at 2:00 a.m., desperately trying to get someone to let me in. It is without a doubt one of the times I've felt the least safe in my travels so far.

10. If you wouldn't do it at home, don't do it when travelling. There are lots of places where random cars or bikes will go past offering you taxi rides, and the number of people who actually use these services is astounding. Most people wouldn't get in an unmarked car or on a bike at home, so don't do it when travelling either.

A Couple in Particular for Women

1. Fall in love with bumbags/fanny packs. Shoulder bags can get you in a lot of trouble and make you a target for scooter snatch-and-grab theft, even if they're across your body.[19]

2. Wear clothes that cover your body when arriving somewhere late at night.

3. Respect cultural norms of clothing; for example, if in India don't walk around in tank tops and shorts, even during the day. Fine if you're in Goa but if you're in the north or travelling around, your life will be so much easier if you just cover up. I know it might be hot but it's definitely worth it.

To stay safe if travelling solo, it is also important to know:

---

[19] The first times I travelled I took a shoulder bag with me and wore it across my body feeling so chuffed with myself that I was being smart and preventing someone from going past on a scooter and snatching it off my shoulder. Having now witnessed one of my friends being dragged along the street by a scooter because her bag was across her body (when they tried to grab it, it didn't come off), I will never do that again. I would much rather someone take my possessions than injure me. So if I were to wear a bag that could go across the body, now I would choose to wear it just on one shoulder. As I'd rather not get injured or lose my possessions if at all possible, I now don't use shoulder bags at all, only bumbags positioned at the front so they would be hard to grab.

Who Are You Going Home with?

And I don't mean whom you are going to bed with.

I mean, if you go to a bar in whichever wonderful place you now find yourself, how are you going to get home?

Are the people you're out with going to want to go home at the same time as you, or are you willing to stay up until they do? Do you know them well enough to know they won't just leave and not think to say bye? Is it safe to walk home? If not, is it safe to get a taxi in that area late at night on your own?

Make sure you know the answers to these questions

If in doubt, ask at the reception of where you're staying.

I've heard some pretty horrible stories as a result of people not knowing the answers to these questions. Don't risk becoming one of them.

Bad things are possible when you travel, but if you are mindful and take precautions such as those suggested above, you can greatly reduce the likelihood of anything happening to you.

Part 5

The Practical Bits

Chapter 15

Planning

Don't Take Away Your Freedom

You need to plan a lot less than you think.

Work out how much you're comfortable with having planned and not planned before leaving for your travels, and then remove about 10-20% of the planning.

Plans can be comforting but can also very quickly end up being constrictive.

My natural tendency is to plan, but the more I travel, the more I realise the only thing over-planning does is ensure you can't be as flexible as you may like. You may be squeezed and time-stressed to get to the next place on your itinerary, and if you decide to change your plans, you'll have to spend money to then cancel reservations made much earlier.

It feels much more liberating and free not to plan too much in advance.

I planned a lot of the first few months of this trip but haven't planned that much since and have had so much more fun.

Over-planning the first months meant that when I was in India, Sri Lanka, and Myanmar I had fun and met some lovely people, but didn't really make any good friends or end up travelling with others at any point, since I couldn't be flexible enough to say, "Yeah, sure, I'll come do that."

Since having fewer plans now, when I've met people who I think are nice I've been able to make plans with them and enjoy travelling together. I've had so much more fun on those parts of my trip and met some incredible people.

Not making plans gives you the freedom to do that.

It gives you the freedom to hear about a place and decide to go there on a whim, or join others for a part of your trip because you enjoy hanging out with them. Most importantly, it means that you will be able to leave if you don't like it, or stay for longer if you do.

My original plans on leaving England had me spending about one month in each of the countries in Asia I was visiting before arriving in Australia by the beginning of August. It's now July of the next year and I'm still in Asia. It's not what I planned but I couldn't be happier with being able to just decide, "Hey, I like it here, I'm going to stay".

Over-planning can also mean that you have to rush from place to place, which means that you'll have technically been to many countries, but you won't have really *seen* them.

When travelling you frequently hear these hideous conversations between people in hostels saying:

"Yeah, well, I've been away two weeks and I've done Vietnam, done Thailand, done Cambodia, and now I'm going to do Laos."

The point of travel isn't so you can say you've been to and "done" a country. The point of travel is to experience new things and places. So give yourself long enough to actually experience each place you're in, rather than treating your travels like a check list of things to tick off.

"Vagabonding[20] is not like bulk shopping; the value of your travels does not hinge on how many stamps you have in your passport when you get home—and the slow nuanced experience of a single country is always better than a hurried superficial experience of forty countries."
Rolf Potts

When you travel, you give yourself the gift of time and freedom, so don't take that away from yourself by planning so much that you no longer have either.[21]

That said, I would always advocate that if you're doing a long-haul flight somewhere for the start of your travels, to book the first night's accommodation in your destination country so you don't have to search around in an unknown city whilst exhausted and jet-lagged.

Having an idea of what you think you might want to do or where you might want to go before leaving

---

[20] "Vagabonding" in this context refers to the activity of travelling long-term.

[21] It is also worth mentioning that it is much better to spend money on doing the interesting things in the locations you're in rather than not doing things so you can save money and have a longer trip, but miss out on the experiences.

home is also by no means a bad thing, but you will have a much better time if you keep it at just that, *an idea*, rather than booking things.

And remember booking anything, including tours, from your home country will be a lot more expensive than doing it when you get there. It's much easier to negotiate in person and with a small company than via email with a large one.

The Practical Things You Have to Plan

There are some things that it is important to plan to some extent as otherwise they will hinder your travels. I've found these to be:

Visas

A lot of countries will require a visa for you to enter and some cannot be bought on arrival; you have to plan ahead and buy the visa before getting to that country.

Before you leave home, look up each of the countries you want to go to or think there is a chance you might visit and write a list of their visa requirements.[22] I have a list like this that I emailed to myself before leaving home so that each time I move, I can double check if I need to do anything in advance in order to be able to enter the next country.

---

[22] If you're from England I found the best website for this was www.gov.uk/foreign-travel-advice. The site also provides information on political situations to be aware of, the safest areas to visit, and a top line overview of health considerations.

Note: I have heard lots of stories of people arriving at border crossings (in places where they issue visas-on-arrival) without any money and then having problems because they can't pay the entrance fee for the visa, and there aren't any ATMs. Always make sure you have the money needed on you to enter the next country at border control. It is very likely there won't be an ATM and border control offices frequently don't accept credit cards.

Vaccinations

It's helpful to have an idea as to the countries you might go to so that you're able to get the appropriate vaccinations before leaving home.

Plan this well in advance as some vaccinations need to be done over a period of time and involve multiple trips to the doctor.

In order to enter a number of countries you will need to have proof of having had a yellow fever vaccination, so make sure you get this done if you will be going to any of these places and take the certificate of your vaccination with you on your travels.[23]

Also check before you leave whether the areas you are travelling to have malaria and that you have the

---

[23] I have the original certificate with me but also have a photocopy, and have taken a photo of it and emailed it to myself, so that if the bag it's in is stolen or lost at any point, I would still have some form of evidence showing I've had the vaccination. I haven't tested out if this would work at border control yet, but it may be enough to get another doctor to reissue the certificate for you wherever you are.

appropriate anti-malaria tablets.[24] Listen to your doctor's advice to try the tablets before you leave. A lot of people have allergic reactions to them, like I did. I got a rash all over my body that was so bad I wanted to peel my own skin off. There's no point having the tablets on you to later discover you can't take them if they don't agree with you.

Plane ticket

Obviously you need a plane ticket to go to your desired destination in the first place, but if you are planning on making multiple stops and going to a lot of countries on your trip, it's worth considering the best way to do this.

You can buy a round-the-world plane ticket with multiple stops.

If you decide to do this, note these things about round-the-world tickets:

- You have to decide in advance which countries you want to go to, in which order, and your preferences might later change.[25]
- When you book a round-the-world ticket you have to book the date and time of each flight in the journey at that time. Whilst most round-the-world tickets allow for free date changes, you

---

[24] I found the NHS Fit For Travel website, www.fitfortravel.nhs.uk, best for this.

[25] I ended up going to Cambodia on this trip, which wasn't part of my original plans, and I had to change the order in which I had planned to visit three countries due to adverse weather conditions, which would have been a lot harder to do if I had a round-the-world ticket since you have to stick to one direction of travel and aren't allowed to go back on yourself.

could end up having to spend a lot of your time on the phone if your plans change significantly in order to move the pre-booked flights.

- Flights are one of the most expensive things to buy while travelling, so a round-the-world ticket does provide peace of mind before leaving that your largest expense is already paid for and you don't have to worry about keeping enough money aside to move from each country to the next or for a flight home at the end.

- Round-the-world tickets are generally cheaper and allow a lot more flexibility in terms of date changes for no extra cost than tickets bought individually.

- Round-the-world plane tickets are only valid for 12 months, so if you decide to stay longer, you could end up losing your flight home, which, given that flights out and back home are the most expensive (rather than the small flights in between), may mean it's not worthwhile for you to get a round-the-world ticket.

I looked extensively at round-the-world tickets before I left the UK, and seeing some of the pre-set routes gave me ideas as to where I might want to travel and what would be the most sensible order.

I didn't end up booking a round-the-world ticket though, because I intended to be away for more than 12 months. Now that I'm travelling, I'm also really happy I didn't book the round-the-world ticket, even if it had lasted for more than 12 months, since things come up, people suggest places to go or do, and with the round-the-world ticket I'd have had much less flexibility to say yes to them without spending more money.

Now I just buy each ticket to the next place as I need it, and it is a lovely feeling knowing that I can leave whenever I want and go elsewhere, as there is nothing I have to stick to. I am completely free.

I can't recommend it enough. However, before you leave make sure you separate off some money into another bank account to cover your airfare home. Better to have that set aside so you know you can always get back at any point if you'd like to.

Power of attorney

Even if you don't think you have anything you'll need looked after for you back home whilst away, it is a very good idea to give someone you know and trust power of attorney for you, just in case.

This is especially true if you own any sort of property.

You can get free templates online to create the document, then just print it out, sign, and leave it with a friend back home.[26]

---

[26] For some purposes the power of attorney document may need to be officially registered (although in a remarkably large number of cases it still suffices without this registration). Registering the document needs to be done with the Office of Public Guardian, if in the UK. The registration takes between 8 to 10 weeks and costs £110. For more information on what giving someone power of attorney means and how to go about it, visit https://www.gov.uk/power-of-attorney/overview.

Travel insurance

It's a good idea to buy travel insurance for your trip, and if you're going away for a long time it can cost a lot of money, so make sure you're prepared for this. It's possible to buy worldwide travel insurance so it doesn't matter if the countries you visit change a bit, but you do need to know if it will include North America and the Caribbean in order to purchase the right type of coverage, if you're from the UK, as they usually make the insurance cost extra.

Chapter 16

What to Pack

There is no need to pack for every possible contingency. Other countries have shops too, and whilst there are some items that can be remarkably hard to find,[27] most things you genuinely need, rather than maybe just want, can be purchased somewhere in whatever country you're in.

Be as ruthless as you can be in your packing. The number of things you need to travel for three weeks really isn't that different from what you need to travel for six months or a year.

Whatever you pack, I can guarantee at some point you will end up dumping some things to free up space in your bag, so don't take anything you will be sad to leave behind. And you may also lose your bag at some point, whether that's through theft or human error.

I thought I'd permanently lost my bag at one point. But I had the happy realisation at that moment in time that I didn't care. It was just clothes. If my bag

---

[27] I forgot to pack nail polish remover; it took me five months to locate a shop that sold it.

had been permanently lost (it wasn't), I'd get the insurance money and buy some more clothes. If you take nothing that you care about, it matters a lot less if you do lose your possessions.

I would also strongly suggest you take a backpack rather than a suitcase on your travels.

There are many instances where you will have to get bags on and off boats or through corridors on trains and having your bag on your back makes life so much easier. It's also a lot easier when you find yourself having to walk for ages to find a hotel—some towns don't have taxis and a 20 minute walk is the only option. I've had to do this with a backpack in a full-on rain storm. A suitcase with wheels would never have made that journey.

Even the largest backpacks don't actually fit that much in and it is wise to be conscious of the weight of your bag when packing. Once you've packed everything into your backpack, make sure you can lift the bag, and if at all possible try to make it light enough that you can lift it over your head. You may have to do this on numerous occasions to get your bag into a luggage rack.

A lot of airlines also charge extra if your bag is more than 15 kg (33 pounds), so that's a very helpful weight to keep under. For this reason I purposefully didn't buy the biggest bag I could, even though I knew I'd be travelling for a long time.

Here are some things I'm extremely happy I didn't leave home without, or wish I had taken with me:

A waterproof cover for your backpack and small rucksack

When I did that 20-minute walk through the rain to my hostel, as there were no taxis in the town, I didn't have a waterproof cover for my backpack. The entire contents of my backpack were soaked and it's kind of hard to find enough space in a dorm room to dry out everything you own.

A torch (flashlight)

There are lots of countries that have planned and un-planned power cuts on a daily basis, so a torch can be incredibly useful. It can also help prevent injury if starting a trek in the dark or walking home when it's dark on uneven dirt roads.

A phone with a standard-sized SIM card

In most countries now, smartphones are everywhere. However they're not all iPhones and finding micro or nano SIM cards can be extremely difficult. Even so, everywhere I've been has always had normal-sized SIM cards readily available.[28]

You may be thinking, what are you doing buying SIM cards in the countries you're going to, anyway? You've spent all this time talking about freedom but then are reconnecting yourself everywhere you go?

---

[28] To ensure the phone you take with you works with these SIMs, make sure it is unlocked before you leave home so you can use any network.

I agree with the questions but there are times when it is incredibly helpful to have a SIM card with internet, and beneficial for your safety.

In India more times than not, I would get in a tuk-tuk or a taxi and have the driver turn around half-way through the journey and not only ask where are we going again, but also where we are. I had to get a SIM to be able to direct the taxi drivers. It also provided some safety in terms of being able to follow the route a driver was taking on Google Maps when journeying in areas, or at times, when it is not the safest for a woman to do so on her own.

Dollars

At all times it is extremely helpful to have at least $100 USD in your bag. I don't mean when going out for an evening, I mean just in your possessions somewhere. American dollars are the most widely accepted currency in the world. Their prevalence will allow you still to make a purchase in most places or can be readily exchanged.

This can help at a border control station in case you get stuck there for any reason, but it's also important as you will unfortunately, at times, find yourself in places where the ATMs just don't work with your bank card, or there is a system error with the ATMs for days, or even no ATMs at all. Always having at least some back-up dollars can get you out of many a sticky situation.

I personally like to keep $100 dollars in my big backpack and also $100 in my small bag. If one bag gets stolen on any journey, I always have some back-up money on me in case of emergency.

Multiple bank cards

Some ATMs in some places just won't accept your bank card. There seems to be no way to predict why or when this will happen, it just does . . . so make sure you take multiple cards from different banks, as some will be rejected whilst others won't.

I have one MasterCard, one Visa card, one Visa debit card, and an American Express card on me. That may sound excessive but each one has helped me greatly at different points in my journey.

The MasterCard is the one I use all the time, as I'm not charged for overseas withdrawals. The Visa card saved me when all my other cards wouldn't work with the ATMs on an island in Thailand. The Visa debit card saved me in two places in Cambodia where the ATMs would only accept debit cards, not credit cards. And the American Express card has proved really helpful for some online bookings, such as trains in India, where either a local bank card was required or an American Express.

Do make sure that at least one of these bank cards won't charge you for transactions abroad.[29] I spent four months in France with a bank card that charged me for every cash withdrawal. It cost me *a lot* of money. Having a card that doesn't charge such fees also means you then don't have to withdraw cash in big chunks. It is much safer to walk around with small amounts than with £200 ($300) on you.

---

[29] If you're from the UK, MoneySavingExpert.com is a great place to find out which cards do and don't charge.

International driving license

I didn't even know this existed when I left England and just assumed I could drive with my license in other countries, but that is not the case everywhere. If you want to drive a scooter or car in a lot of countries you will need an international driving license as well as your standard one, or you'll have to pay a lot of fines.[30]

There are two types of international driving licenses that cover different countries, so check which one you need or just get both to be on the safe side, in case your plans change.

---

[30] If you're from England, you can get these via the Post Office, http://www.postoffice.co.uk/international-driving-permit, and they only cost £5.50. Given the popularity of scooters as a method of transport in a lot of countries I'd also suggest learning how to drive one in the familiar setting of your home town before leaving. To drive a scooter in the UK you will need to complete a Compulsory Basic Training (CBT) course. The courses are usually one day long. Further information can be found at https://www.gov.uk/cbt-compulsory-basic-training.
It is also worth noting that traffic laws are different in most countries, as are driving customs. For example, in the US drivers can directly turn right at a red traffic light (the equivalent of a left-hand turn in the UK) but in the UK for the equivalent turn the driver would not be allowed to go through the red light. In some countries there is little to no traffic control at big intersections, therefore local customs have been adopted to ensure everyone knows what they're doing, such as, in many countries hazard lights are put on to indicate that you will be continuing straight across a junction. Given this, it is worthwhile researching the traffic laws in any country you plan to drive in and then observing what others do when out on the road.

Passport photos

A lot of visa applications will require passport photos. To save yourself time and hassle, just take a lot with you. I left home with 12 copies of my passport photo, and I'm very happy I did.

Passport

Obviously you're going to need your passport, but is your passport as you need it to be for your trip? Will it have more than six months left of validity for the whole of your trip? Do you have a lot of blank pages side by side left? If the answer is "no" to either of these questions, renew your passport before leaving home. Lots of countries require more than six months validity and two to three consecutive blank pages for entry. I had to renew mine before leaving, so opted to get a double-size passport with 48 pages rather than 24, to ensure I would have no issues—and it's filling up fast!

Make sure you carry with you some photocopies of your passport photo page and any visas you have.[31] I personally stash at least one in each bag just in case. Bear in mind there are some countries in the world where if you're stopped by police and can't show at least a photocopy of your passport and visa they can technically take you to jail (most likely you'll just have

---

[31] There are some countries where a photocopy won't suffice and you have to, by law, have your passport on you at all times. It is worth checking the regulations regarding this for each country you intend to visit. A good source of this information is Lonely Planet: www.lonelyplanet.com.

to throw a lot of money at the situation but better to avoid it altogether if you can).

Entertainment

Most of the time while travelling you'll be out seeing amazing things or hanging out with others, so you won't often need to worry about how you'll entertain yourself.

However there are very likely to be some 16-hour train rides or 20-hour bus rides at some point in your travels if you're on a budget. And they can get boring if you have nothing to entertain yourself with, or annoying if it's too noisy to sleep but you don't even have any music to drown the noise out.

For this reason I am extremely happy I brought my Kindle and iPod with me.

The Kindle is great because it means I have loads of books to read whenever I want without lugging around heavy paperbacks. And I don't have to hunt for books in my own language when I finish one and want another.

The iPod is wonderful as I can play music if where I'm staying or a journey is noisy. Also I can listen to podcasts on it. I'd never listened to a podcast before travelling, but some of them are fascinating, and great on a bumpy bus ride. By bumpy, I mean *really* bumpy. I've been on some bus rides where you're literally flying out of your seat, having to hold onto the one in front for dear life, and it's not possible to read. If you get travel sick, this will be an even bigger issue. Podcasts or audio books can be great.

DEET mosquito spray

Whilst you can get mosquito spray in most places, it can be hard to find strong mosquito spray with a high percentage of DEET. Whilst I don't really mind getting bitten by mosquitoes that much, if it's an area with dengue fever or malaria I'd really like to have DEET mosquito spray on me. I save it for those areas, though, and just use the weaker sprays, if at all, in the other areas.

Sudocrem

Yes, the nappy rash cream. Judge me all you want, but that stuff is amazing.

It works on rashes, sunburn, cuts, and as an antiseptic. It's the most useful and versatile medicinal item I have with me.

Also, you may actually want it for nappy rash. With long sweaty bus rides and hours spent sitting around in wet swim clothes at times, nappy rash happens to a lot of people when travelling.

Padlocks

Most hostels will provide at least a small space to lock your valuables in, with many even providing a larger locker for your whole backpack as well. They frequently don't provide padlocks, though, so be sure to take a couple with you on your travels.

Tampons

One for the ladies, clearly. If you like using tampons I'd strongly recommend packing at least a box or two to take with you at the start of your travels. In some countries it can be extremely hard to find tampons (if not impossible) and in others they are just ridiculous expensive. In Indonesia they're £18 ($27) a pack. *£18!* Lastly when packing, make sure you:

Leave space

Whatever you pack there will be some things you didn't think of that you need or clothing that you realise you'll be more comfortable in once you get to your destination. It's really important to leave space in your bag in case you need to buy any items on the way.

Chapter 17

Jump in the Deep End or Step-by-Step?

You don't need to, and shouldn't, plan your whole trip out, but you do need to work out where you're going to start.

If you haven't travelled before, an important question to ask yourself is how you like to do things in life? Are you a jump-straight-in, sink-or-swim kind of person, or do you prefer to take things gradually and ease yourself into them?

The answer to this question will be a large factor in deciding where you should start your travels.

If you prefer to ease yourself into things gradually in life and haven't travelled that much before, it's a good idea to start your travels in a country similar to your own in some regards. If you're from England or the US, somewhere in Europe or Australia would be a good place to start. You'll still have rich, varied experiences in these countries, but it will be less of an initial shock arriving in them. Modes of transport may be different to what you're used to at home; for example, if you go to Croatia you'll spend most of your time on boats, and languages will still vary. But a location like this will give you a great place to get your bearings and work out your travel groove before moving on to other places that have greater differences and are harder to get around.

Thailand can also provide a great starting point for those wanting to ease themselves into travel but not wanting to start in a Western country. There is a lot of tourism in Thailand so whilst it's still possible to have authentic experiences and view some incredible things there, getting around, finding accommodation, meeting others, and travel in general is much easier than in a lot of neighbouring countries.

Personally I've always been a fan of the sink-or-swim method in life, so one of the first places I ever travelled around was Vietnam.

Arriving there the first night and trying to cross the road was a huge shock. There were about 100 scooters swarming in different directions showing no sign of looking like they'd stop, *ever*. I was with a friend and we both looked at each other in horror, thinking how are we going to cross the road? Then we spotted a local, so decided to follow them as they just walked straight out into the road letting the scooters swerve expertly around them as they went.

Travelling round Vietnam was tough at times. But it did mean I was much better prepared to handle anything when I went to other countries afterward.

I started this trip I'm now on in India, and had I not been to Vietnam before I probably would have been freaked out on seeing the traffic. Instead all I thought was "Pfff, that's nothing in comparison to Vietnam. I've got this."

If you decide to go for sink-or-swim and throw yourself into a country that is harder to negotiate straight off, it will make other countries that are easier to travel feel like a walk in the park or a little holiday. But there is no right or wrong way, just whichever way suits how you like to do things best.

Chapter 18

Accommodation and Flights

Accommodation

It is a lot cheaper not to book accommodation until you arrive in each destination. This is because accommodation prices are usually very much negotiable.

If you can, it is therefore better to just arrive somewhere and find accommodation once you do. You'll have a heavy bag on you, so it's worth researching a few places you like the look of first, so you know the areas to try. But you'll usually find that most budget accommodation is in a similar area so it's easy to walk from one hostel to the next to ask about prices.[32]

---

[32] If you're going to a busy location, or somewhere without a lot of accommodation options, using this method does come with a risk of places being booked up, therefore I'd suggest being mindful of this when choosing where to arrive with no pre-set plans.

A huge benefit of this method is also that you can see the place before booking, meaning you won't accidentally find yourself in a squalid pit. And to continue the advice on not over-planning, when you get there just book a night or two. That way you can keep extending if you want, but have the freedom to go whenever you would like.

Types of Accommodation

Hostels

I list these first as they're the most popular type of accommodation for travellers, given their affordability. Hostels provide good value for money, are set up to make it much easier to meet others than hotels (where you're all separated off into private rooms with no communal areas). Hostels have gotten a bad reputation over the years and if you haven't stayed in one recently they might conjure images of dirty, cramped accommodation, but for the most part *this is not the case.* Most hostels are clean, with plenty of amenities and ample space. Standard facilities are even reaching the stage now where all beds, if in a dorm, come with a private lamp, plug socket, and a lockable storage space for all of your luggage. Some hostels I've stayed in have been nicer than hotels, with pools, rooftop views, and amazing bars.

Common features of hostels include:
- Both dorm and private rooms
- A common area
- Free breakfast
- Information about the local area

- A bar with discount drinks promotions
- Lockers, both for smaller valuable items and for backpacks
- Free wi-fi
- Laundry service

Hotels

Less popular with travellers but with hotel rooms costing as little as a pound or two in some areas, or there being no hostels in particular locations, anyone travelling for a while will probably stay in a hotel at some point.

I wouldn't recommend staying in a hotel for all of your travels unless you are travelling with another person and really have no interest in meeting other people. Hotels are just not set up to be as social as hostels. It is also worth noting that some cheaper hotels will have much worse living conditions than a hostel for the same price.

Common features of hotels include:

- Private rooms
- Breakfast, free or for an additional cost
- Information about the local area
- A restaurant and bar
- A safe for smaller valuable items
- Wi-fi, sometimes free but frequently at an extra cost

Homestays

Frequently when homestay is listed next to an accommodation option, it means nothing more than that it is a low-cost hotel or a hotel that is owned by people from the area.

Homestay should mean staying with a family from the local area, therefore (when the description is accurate) the accommodation will either be someone's house or a slightly larger set up that verges on a hotel but is much more personal and friendly. As with hotels, homestays can make it harder to meet other travellers. However, if it is a true homestay, the owners are likely to take you under their wing and show you around a bit or at the very least teach you about the culture of the area.

Common features of homestays include:

- Private rooms
- Free breakfast
- Information on the local area, including both touristy and less touristy activities
- Tour guiding services
- Rental of items frequently required in that area, for example, scooters

There is another type of homestay available that doesn't always involve the owner being there, which is Airbnb. Airbnb is a website on which houses or rooms are listed for rent by their owners at cheaper rates than you would usually find for hotels. This can be perfect if you'd like to spend a while in a location and have accommodation that will feel more like your own. It can be much more time consuming to arrange accommodation via Airbnb, however, so I would advise using it only for stays of more than a couple of days.

Free accommodation

It is possible to find accommodation for free due to the kindness of strangers who list their couches and spare rooms for those passing through an area. Couchsurfing.com is one example of where accommodation like this can be found. Staying with a couch-surfing host is completely free. All you have to do is go onto the website and search the dates you will be in a specific area to find the options of those offering up their homes for guests to stay in.

Since it is free this is an extremely popular option with travellers. There are measures in place on the site to help ensure the safety of those staying in these strangers' houses, such as all users have to have a profile that gives information about them and you can look at reviews from previous guests.

I have, though, never used this option myself. I am a female travelling on my own and whilst I have met numerous people who have had wonderful experiences with couch surfing, meeting people who are still their friends to this day, I don't feel comfortable staying in a stranger's house on my own. If I were travelling with others I would, but on my own, for me personally, the potential risk is not worth the benefit. That said, if you are comfortable with it, couch surfing can be a great way to save some money.

Researching and Choosing Your Accommodation

When researching hostels and hotels, or if you are going to book in advance as you know you're going to a particularly busy location, the sites I find best for this are Booking.com and Hostelworld.com.

Booking.com is always my first port of call, as it has an easy-to-use map view of the accommodation, allows free cancellation a lot of the time, and cancellations can even be made on their website without having to call the hostel (very helpful if you're not yet in that country).

Sometimes Booking.com lacks on the hostel options in a particular location (you'll know if this is the case if you can't find anything with a dorm room when searching), so then I look on Hostelworld.com as they usually have the most hostels; the functionality of the site is just a lot less user friendly.

If you haven't looked for hostels or cheap budget hotels online before, here are some things to look out for:

Location
- Always look at the map view, try to work out the whereabouts of the centre of town, the main attractions, nightlife (if you're interested in it), and the area with most of the other accommodation in that town.

Rating and reviews
- Always check the hostel's rating to see what others thought of it and read a couple of the reviews.

From the reviews you will easily be able to tell if the rating is fair or not. I've read numerous reviews where the complaints have been things like, "They didn't carry my bag to my room", or "There was a noisy person in my dorm". The first of these doesn't bother me and the second is just bad luck, so it's worth checking if the reviews are things that actually matter to you or not.

Amenities

- Do they have lockers, air conditioning, a common room or bar, etc.? In some countries it really matters if there is air con because a dorm room with only a fan can feel like a sauna, so it's worth checking. I mention a common room or bar, because if you're travelling solo it's much better to stay in hostels with these facilities as they make it a lot easier to meet people.

Flights

One of the best resources I've ever been introduced to for saving money on flights is the month view option on Skyscanner.com.

On Skyscanner you can put in your departure point and arrival point (the arrival point can be as broad as a whole country), and then select a whole month you want to see the prices for, or even select any time. This brings up a graph which you can scroll through to pick the cheapest day to travel, and if you've searched by country, the cheapest airport to fly into as well.

Momondo.com is another site that provides a similar graph view feature to check the cheapest dates to travel, and allows searches to be conducted using nearby airports as well as the ones you have specified.

If you're heeding the advice in Chapter 15 and not planning too much in advance, these date-view search functions will be perfect for you. Since you don't have plans already set, it doesn't matter which exact day you travel, so just pick the cheapest option.

Tripdelta.com is also a very handy site for planning flights if you have a specific destination and date you need to travel there. Tripdelta.com will search the exact route you've put in but then also bring up options of other routes that would be cheaper or faster to the same destination.

If possible I would recommend booking the flights with the airlines directly once you've found the option you want. That way you know you definitely have the ticket and it's easier to make any changes because you can talk directly to the airline if you need to.[33]

---

[33] It's not always assured that you have the plane ticket if you buy through a third party, as they have to ask for the ticket to be issued on your behalf. Once when I booked through Opodo.com, they "forgot" to do this, leaving me sitting at the airport with no ticket. I discovered online afterwards many other instances of this happening to others, too. I now only book with airlines directly.

Part 6

Attitude to Travel

Chapter 19

Care a Little Less

"As new experiences and insights take you in surprising new directions, you'll gradually come to understand why long-time travellers insist that the journey itself is far more important than any destination."
Rolf Potts

It will be extremely beneficial for the enjoyment of your travels to care a little bit less when on the road. That may seem like a strange thing to say given I've been talking about how travelling allows you to see and do lots of wonderful things, but I'm not talking about not caring about *what* you're doing. Just learning to stop caring, or caring less, about the things that don't matter.

Travel is not just filled with beautiful views and amazing experiences one after the other. There are long travel days in between, a lot of organising that has to be done at times, and any number of scams or potentially frustrating things that can happen. As a result travel is so much more enjoyable if you can

109

learn to be a bit more relaxed about these things and remember what is actually important.

It may well be that the cost changes of something you'd previously agreed to, your bag is lost, or you arrive six hours later than you were meant to. Sure, you don't want to be ripped off or walked all over, but there is only a certain extent to which these things matter.

For example, if the price of something you'd agreed to is changed by £1 ($1.50) at the last minute, yes, by all means try to explain that's not right. However, don't make yourself angry and waste the rest of your day arguing about it. The only person you are screwing over if you do that is yourself.

> *"Choose not to be harmed, and you won't feel harmed.*
> *Don't feel harmed, and you haven't been."*
> **Marcus Aurelius**

Similarly with journeys being delayed (this happens frequently). I have watched so many friends get extremely angry about delays when arriving places, be that because our bus broke down or a boat was stuck outside a harbour for hours. The thing is, getting angry about this and complaining about it isn't going to change anything. You're still going to arrive at the same time. And yeah, you may have lost half a day in your next destination, but so what? What you bought yourself in going travelling is time. That is the thing you now have, so it doesn't matter that much if you lose half a day. Just relax, go back to what you were doing before the delay, be that reading, sleeping, or writing, and try to enjoy it.[34]

I love reading books and sometimes don't get to as much I'd like, as I get distracted by doing other activities. So for me a bus delay isn't really such a bad thing, it's just more reading time.

Find out what is the thing you enjoy doing and could do on long journeys, and it will make any delays much more enjoyable.

Also it's important to remember that all those holdups are part of the experience.

"We are often so caught up in our destination that we forget to appreciate the journey, especially the goodness of the people we meet on the way."
Anonymous

In Cambodia, if you take a bus journey that's only six-hours, it's likely to stop three times, two of which are for sit-down meals, which still boggles my mind somewhat. Without those stops the journey would probably take four hours, but the focus is on making the journey an enjoyable experience. They're in no rush to get there. And neither should you be. At those stops on the journey you have time to get to know the other people on the bus and have dinner with groups of both locals and foreigners whom you may otherwise not have met.

There will also be times when you're looking for a bus or the like and end up having to get on one, but

---

[34] Since a delay in one part of a journey could cause a missed connection, check that the provider you would like to use for travel insurance will cover the cost of this.

aren't really sure if it's the *right* bus. When you do, instead of sitting there stressing whether you're going to reach your desired destination, ask yourself: does it really matter if you do? If you haven't over-planned your trip, then all it means is you end up somewhere else for a day. And who knows, that new place may be even more of a fun adventure than what you'd originally planned.

Have an open mind and consider how whatever happens is just part of the adventure. You'll have a lot more fun.

As well as caring a bit less about things not going to plan, it will also serve you well to accept before you go away that the standards of things such as accommodation and toilets are likely to be a different than what you're used to back home, if you're going to a non-Western country.

So keep in mind what is actually important in those things.

For accommodation, even a simple place is fine as long as it's reasonably clean, provides a roof over your head, and is safe. That's really all you need. Sure, a fancy hotel can be nice once in a while but some of the most basic places actually turn out to be most fun. Generally the people who stay in the unfussy accommodation options are more relaxed and friendly, since their focus isn't on luxuries but instead on the experience.

If you're used to a high standard of living, this may take a while to get used to, so ease yourself into it over time.

Toilets are also likely to be very different and not have the same standard of cleanliness that you're used to.

First of all learn to tell the difference between a toilet being no-frills and being unclean. I went to a toilet in Laos where a guy came out saying, "Oh my God, it's so disgusting in there. There's a giant bucket of water and you have to scoop the water out with a ladle to put down the toilet to flush it."

I almost burst out laughing.

It's extremely common for toilets to be like that in Asia and the rest of the bathroom was lovely and clean. It made me wonder how he was going to survive the rest of his trip if he thought that bathroom was disgusting.

Lots of bathrooms have the bucket and ladle to use instead of a flush button and many are also squat toilets,[35] which can mean there's a lot of water on the floor, but they're not necessarily unclean.

Many toilets are located out the back of restaurants or bars down little dirt tracks (the toilet at my favourite bar in Costa Rica was like this, which always made for a fun trip to the loo, trying to dodge pebbles and rogue geckos!). Some toilets just aren't actually really toilets at all; instead there's a rock on the floor in a closed off space, a grass area, or even just a hole cut out of the floor of a house so you can squat and pee into the ground below.

Again, this is where it's important to remember what's important. In terms of toilets, you need to be able to do your business and that's it. If the toilet provides you with a space to do that, then your basic needs have been met.

---

[35] Squat toilets are on the ground, and instead of having a toilet seat to sit on, have a space either side of the toilet hole to place your feet and squat over.

You may want to carry some toilet paper on you and possibly disinfectant hand gel, depending on how likely you think you are to get grossed out by toilets not looking particularly clean. But a less than perfect toilet in general isn't going to do you any harm.

There are also a lot of situations when travelling where you won't be able to get the food you would like to eat, or don't have a choice but to eat whatever's there.

At one point in my travels I have found myself stuck in the middle of a tiny town, in a thunderstorm where there was only one place that sold food. I don't even think it was a restaurant, just someone's house, but there happened to be one person eating some food there so it was by far our most viable option to try. Since it wasn't actually a restaurant, there wasn't a menu of any description and none of us spoke the language, so the only way we could order was to point to the bowl the one other person had and make hand gestures to indicate eating. Which would have been fine, except that I don't eat meat. A much longer, more intricate mime therefore ensued to try to explain with no words that I would like no meat in my meal. We must have looked ridiculous but for one glorious moment we thought it had worked. The woman smiled at us and fired something rapidly back at us in the local language, pointing to my friend and then to me indicating she understood we both wanted something different.

Turns out it didn't work. Who knows what she thought we'd been trying to say but we definitely didn't manage to convey the message we'd been intending and I still ended up with meat in my meal.

It's situations like this when you need to remember what's important. Sometimes you just need to eat. It may not be what you want to eat, and may even have things in it you don't usually eat, but just eat as much as you need to not be hungry anymore, and pick out the bits you don't like. It's not ideal but better than going hungry.[36]

---

[36] If you have a number of allergies, it would be very good idea to take some snacks with you anywhere you go, just in case.

Chapter 20

Learn to Haggle

In many parts of the world haggling is part of the norm. This is especially true in areas with markets where there are no fixed prices displayed so shop-keepers can tell potential customers whatever price they like. The customer can then either decide to accept this price, walk away, or start negotiating for a lower price.

The shopkeeper expects the customer to negotiate for a lower price, though, so will have made their first price much higher than it should be, especially if they've decided the customer looks rich or slightly naïve.

For some people the thought of haggling is horrible, seeing it as a tense, uncomfortable conversation. But it doesn't have to be.

Bear in mind the shopkeepers you're haggling with do this every day. They won't see it as insulting, it's the norm, even part of the culture in a lot of places.

It is important that you do haggle and learn to get more comfortable with it, otherwise you will be ripped off wherever you go.

The difference between the starting price of some items and the price you buy it at can be astronomical.

In India, for example, when looking at scarves I was told the ones I liked were £20 ($30). I ended up buying them for £3 ($4.50) each.

Similarly when a friend of mine arrived in the Philippines, the first taxi they asked the price of said £30 ($45). The journey should cost £3 ($4.50).

While travelling there will be times you will need to haggle for pretty much anything and everything. I've haggled for clothes, boat tickets, hotels, scooter prices, language schools, treks, taxis, water sports, and even a beer at one point.

There is an important rule to remember when haggling, though. Just as as you don't want to get ripped off, you shouldn't go in wanting to rip the other person off, either. The aim is to get a fair price for the item you're buying, so you both walk away from the transaction happy.

Don't be that person who stands there for 20 minutes haggling over 20p (30¢). If the shopkeeper has dug their heels in that much, it's probably because they've reached the point at which they're not making enough money from the sale at a lower price. And bear in mind that 20p probably means a lot more to them than it does to you.

Tips for Haggling

1. Always be willing to walk away. If you're not willing to let the item go if the price doesn't move enough, you will most likely end up paying more than you should for it.

2. Do actually walk away and say you're going to have a look around or think. As soon as your feet start moving towards the door nine times out of ten the shopkeeper will throw a string of lower prices at you to stop you from leaving.

3. If number 2 happens but you're still not sure about the price, say again you're going to think about it and leave this time. There are two things you can then do:

   - Go to the shop next door that probably has identical stock, tell them the price you were offered, and see if they'll beat it. You could then go back to the original shop, but again remember don't push it so far you rip someone off. *Or*

   - Don't go to the next shop but just go back to the original shop five minutes later with the amount you are willing to pay in exact cash in your hand. Hold it out to the shopkeeper whilst saying how much you're willing to pay. If they don't take it, the item is not for sale at that price. It's much harder for someone to refuse a sale if the cash is right there in front of them, so unless you really have pushed the price too low they will probably accept the offer.

4. When it comes to haggling for a taxi, tuk-tuk, or whatever mode of transport you're taking, make sure you do it up front. You've lost your bargaining power by the end of the journey. Never get in a taxi or the like without first agreeing on the price. And

make sure you have small change or the negotiating may not have been worth it, since they may claim, or actually not have, any small money for change. If the taxis in the area you are in have meters, insist it's turned on and be willing to wait a couple of taxis to find one that will use the meter.[37] If the taxis all still refuse to use the meter, offer to pay a small amount over the meter price so the taxi driver is still getting more than normal but you know that you won't be hugely overcharged.

Given the prevalence of haggling in many parts of the world, this causes certain situations to be a lot more intense and pressured than they would be back home. For example, when you get off a train instead of being able to calmly walk to a taxi rank and get in, knowing you will get a fair price, you are instead likely to be swarmed by 30 or so drivers all shouting different prices at you, trying to grab your bag to put in their vehicle and secure your custom.

When this happens you need to be firm. Never let someone bully you into going with them or accepting a higher price than you should just because you're overwhelmed by the clamour of people.

It is absolutely fine to tell them you need a minute and to stop grabbing your bag. Don't be aggressive, but be assertive. A lot of theft happens in crowds of people like this. If you feel in any way uncomfortable or people are invading your personal space, just tell them to back away. Much better to do that than to say nothing and risk something bad happening.

---

[37] In many countries it is very common for taxi drivers to refuse to use the meter if you're foreign, hence why it may take a few tries to get one who agrees to do so.

Chapter 21

Do Things That Scare You

"Sometimes all you need is 20 seconds of insane courage;
20 seconds of embarrassing bravery."
Benjamin Mee

It may be that the idea of going on this trip scared you at first, but once you're on your way, you will no doubt have an amazing time. So keep that adventurous and brave spirit with you as you travel. Don't be reckless but do push yourself out of your comfort zone.

That might be by trying new things that seem weird to you, like eating with your hand,[38] or taking part in activities that scare you, like haggling or a sport you've always been afraid of.

---

[38] Note if you try this, only do so with your right hand, even if it's not your dominant hand. The left hand is used for wiping when going to the toilet in a lot of countries, so it's seen as un-clean to eat with your left.

Even if certain customs seem completely bizarre to you or terrifying at first, give them a go. You might end up liking some of them.

For example, in most of Asia when you go to the toilet you'll find a hose with a water gun spout on the top, commonly known as a "bum gun". People use it to clean after going to the bathroom.

I have met so many people who now can't begin to work out how they're going to cope with just using paper again when they get back home, they've fallen so in love with this strange contraption that confused them at first.

I personally would never have discovered scuba diving if it weren't for having gone on my travels with this attitude of trying things that scare me, since I've always had a fear of swimming around lots of fish. They move so fast, and there are so many of them that it's always caused me to panic when I find myself surrounded by them in the water. But after months of making myself go snorkelling whenever the opportunity arose I finally became comfortable enough to try scuba diving, which is genuinely one of the most incredible things I've ever done. So much so that I not only now scuba dive, but went so far as to do my open water and advanced qualifications. Getting over the fear was 100% worth now being able to explore the beautiful hidden world beneath the sea.

As mentioned in Chapter 8, about travelling alone, use travel as an opportunity to grow.

Have a think about the things you're scared of and try to push yourself out of your comfort zone to try them. You might discover something you love in the process.

Chapter 22

What to Do While You're Travelling

"Change is inevitable but personal growth is a choice."
Bob Proctor

There is nothing wrong with going to travel with no other aim than to go to another country and see what you find there.

Bear in mind though that just seeing monument after monument will probably get tiring after some time. There is such a thing as temple fatigue and it's very real.

Doing the same thing over and over again will not create the most enjoyable travel experience.

If we do anything numerous times then it gets boring, no matter what the activity is.

So have an idea of something else that interests you, something you might be able to find in a few of the countries you go to that will make your experience all the richer.

For example, I started my travels deciding I wanted to learn things. I made that my theme. So in the different countries I've been to, I've looked each time to find something there I'd like to learn. In India I learnt yoga, in Thailand scuba diving, in Indonesia surfing and the Indonesian language, and I plan to learn capoeira in Brazil.

I don't have to do any of these things, and there have been countries where all I've done is sightsee; my time is still totally free to do whatever I want with it. But the times I decided to learn things have been some of the most enjoyable and rich parts of my trip.

I've always loved learning, so this was a natural choice for me. For you it may be a love of starting projects, or helping others, or photography, or writing. Consider whether there is anything that would bring you happiness on top of your travels, or that could even help you with deciding the countries you wish to visit, such as where aid is most needed, or where they teach that specific sport you've always wanted to learn.

I would personally recommend learning the language in at least one country you visit. Learning another language while immersed in that place will give you much greater insight and depth of understanding into the culture.[39]

---

[39] For this reason I have gone to language school in Spain, France, Costa Rica, and Indonesia. You can learn languages by picking them up on the street and there are a lot of good apps that will help give you a kick start in your desired language, but attending a language school is by far the quickest way to do this. Once you've got the basics it's then much easier to pick up new words as you go about your daily life in that country but it can be very hard to pick things up with no understanding to begin with. Language school will also give you the quickest cultural insight into the place you are in, since many of the discussions used for learning will centre around topics relevant to the area.

"It is impossible to understand a culture without understanding its language.... Gain a language and you gain a second lens through which to question and understand the world. Cursing at people when you go home is fun, too."
Tim Ferriss

"Learning another language is not only learning different words for the same things, but learning another way to think about things."
Flora Lewis

Plus, it's also really enjoyable. I was dreadful at languages at school but learning a language in the country in which it's spoken is much easier and faster. And once you learn one it makes others much easier to learn.

Another activity worth trying could be writing a journal. I've met a lot of people who have discovered that they really enjoy keeping a journal of their experiences whilst travelling. The only thing I'd warn about with this is to not get so caught up in writing it that you miss out on experiencing half of each day because you're writing about the other half. If there are fun, interesting things to go do, go do them, and write later.

Travelling is a very organic process. Because you don't have lots of distractions you'll listen to yourself more, and more often than not just know what you want to do next and what would make you happiest.

So make sure you're paying attention.

Choose Your Life

"Never leave that till tomorrow which you can do today."
Benjamin Franklin

If you want to travel, don't keep putting it off and telling yourself you'll do it in the future. Make the decision to do it now and start working towards it.

The set of circumstances in which it would be the perfect time to travel aren't magically going to present themselves. You have to create them.

"Change will not come if we wait for some other person, or if we wait for some other time. We are the ones we've been waiting for. We're the change that we seek."
Barak Obama

You have nothing to lose, and everything to gain.

If you would like to read more about how to enable your travels and keep up to date with my journey, visit www.TravelForYourLife.com. Here you will find further information on the topics discussed in this book and additional tools and resources to help you on your travels.

If you have enjoyed this book, I would be extremely grateful if you would post a review of your thoughts on Amazon. Most people don't bother to leave reviews but it would mean so much to me if you would take two minutes to do so. I personally read every one and would love to hear your thoughts.

Bonus Material

Top Tips on Selected Destinations

This book isn't designed to be a travel guide, so I haven't included full, detailed information on the places I've visited. However there are a couple of small points that I found really helpful to know, or learnt the hard way, about some of the countries I've been to recently. These are all countries in Asia, as that's where I've spent the last couple of years.

India

Taxis can be dangerous in India, especially for women on their own. To help protect yourself when you get a taxi ask the driver for their phone number, and take a picture of the license plate. All phone numbers in India are registered, so they'll know that you now have access to all their details and will assume you've sent the photo to a friend, so they will get busted if they try anything. I'm not saying this is a foolproof method; in general try to avoid taxis on your own where possible and especially at night.

To book a train ticket online in India you need a local bank card or an American Express credit card.

Once you've got over that hurdle, be sure to pay attention to the codes used next to the seats you're being sold. WL means waitlist and doesn't actually mean you have a seat. There will be a number next to WL as well, so it could say "WL (18)" for example. That means you will actually only have a seat on that train if 18 people cancel before you. I learnt this lesson the hard way, as they still send you a confirmation text of your booking so it appears very much as if you have a ticket for that journey, but you don't if you're on the waitlist.

Sri Lanka

You need to be able to show you have a flight booked to leave the country in order to enter.

The distances between most places in Sri Lanka aren't that far, especially in comparison to places like India, but what should be a three-hour journey can and frequently does take all day due to having to take multiple buses or trains that stop frequently and don't allow a straight path to your next destination. Allow plenty of time to get between places in Sri Lanka.

Laos

In a number of bars in Laos, as well as being handed a drinks menu, you will be handed a drugs menu. *Don't buy the drugs.* This isn't a "don't do drugs, kids" message, you're adults, you can choose to do whatever you want. However, if you buy drugs in Laos it is very likely a scam where you won't actually get to take them and will instead end up $200-$300 down from having to pay off the police.

The bars and dealers sell the drugs to tourists and then tip off the police so that even if people go back to their hotels to do the drugs, the police will appear there five minutes later and bust them. Yeah, you're probably not going to go to jail as all the police want is a "fine", but do you really want to spend $300 for a joint?

Myanmar

It used to be that there were no ATMs in Myanmar that would accept international bank cards. That is no longer the case, however they are few and far between so take cash. Just to be safe, take as much as you think you need for the whole time you are there and then take some more.

In order to be able to exchange money in Myanmar you need to take American dollars, but all the bills must be new notes and must not have any markings, tears, or folds. I mean *any*. I knew this when travelling there and so had checked the bank notes I was given and yet still found myself with three $100 bills that no one would exchange.

Buses between destinations in Myanmar are frequently booked up, making it next to impossible to decide spontaneously to go somewhere and actually be able to leave that day. Always book a day or two in advance.

I would strongly recommend the night buses there. They're really comfortable and a much nicer experience than travelling through the day in the sweltering heat on buses that are much more cramped.

Thailand

Thailand offers visas on arrival, however if you're from the UK and apply for a visa at home before going, you can get a six-month triple-entry visa. Because of where Thailand is located in relation to a lot of other countries in Asia, this can be extremely handy as you may find yourself passing through multiple times.

Indonesia

Most foreigners are now able to get a free entry visa on arrival for 30 days.[40] However, if you think there is a chance you will stay more than 30 days, do not take that visa. You will have to leave the country after 30 days and come back in again.

If you want to stay longer than 30 days, stop at the visa-on-arrival desk and pay the $35 dollars for the visa. You will then be able to extend within the country for another 30 days.

---

[40] This free entry visa is only available at certain airports. If you accept it, then there are only five airports from which you can then leave the country, you are not allowed to depart from any other. Currently those airports are: Soekarno Hatta – Tangerang, Ngurah Rai – Bali, Kualanamu – Medan, Surabaya – Juanda, and Hang Nadim – Batam. If you're not sure where you're going to want to fly out of, it's therefore much better to pay for the standard visa-on-arrival.

Useful Apps

There are some apps that can make travelling around much easier and remove a lot of difficulties that otherwise might be faced. Here's a round up of a few that are particularly useful:

Google Translate

I quite enjoy not having a clue what things say and having to figure it out via gestures and pantomime to the person you're trying to communicate with. However, you don't actually need to do this now days.

The Google Translate app now includes a word lens so you can hold it over any writing and it will automatically translate the text. Kind of spoils the fun of trying to order a vegetarian meal when you understand nothing on the menu for me, but it can make life a lot easier. Languages can be downloaded in the app so that it will work offline.

XE Currency Conversion

I work out a rough multiple for the exchange rate in each place I go to so that it's easy to convert costs, but if you move from country to country this can quickly become hard. This is where an app from a company like XE can come in handy. I always use XE.com when checking exchange rates anyway, as it is known to be one of the most accurate. If you have a phone that will allow you to download the app, this could save a lot of time.

Google Maps

The Google Maps app can be so helpful as if you load the map of the location you're in whilst you have connection to the internet. Then when you leave that internet connection the map will still continue to work on your device, and even track where you are with a blue dot.

Flickr

You're likely to be taking a lot of photos whilst travelling around. In case any of your electronic items are stolen, it's sensible to back up photos as quickly as possible. Flickr offers a terabyte of storage, which is huge, absolutely free, and it's easy to upload photos and keep them all private.

There are lot of other sites that offer this service too, however it's very hard to find this much storage for free elsewhere.

Uber

Uber exists in a surprisingly large number of countries, and when located in places where it's hard or expensive to get taxis, Uber can be extremely useful. Do bear in mind, though, if you're using Uber that they don't screen their drivers. Therefore safety should be considered.

In most places there will be a local version of Uber as well, so ask around and see the app most others are using in that location to get taxis (or even in some places motorbike taxis).

About the Author

Chantell Glenville, BA (Hons), quit her job to travel in 2014 and has been on the road ever since.

She has travelled countless times before, sometimes spending long periods of time in one place or country, and at other times constantly moving from place to place quickly. Her travels so far have taken her to Central America, South America, Asia, Western Europe, and Eastern Europe.

During her travels she has also written and published *What Clients Really Want (And The S**t That Drives Them Crazy)*, an essential guide for anyone in client-services on how to create great client relationships.

Chantell has been featured in various national and international publications, and won the WACL Future Leaders Award in 2013.

She is the founder of JY Marketing Consultancy, which offers top-level training on marketing, from how to create a brand to communications strategy and creating effective marketing campaigns

To find out more about Chantell and her other areas of interests (there are *a lot*), visit chantellglenville.com or contact her on chantell@chantellglenville.com.

Acknowledgements

This book is dedicated to all those who dream they could travel, since I believe there is no other experience that will have as beneficial an effect on someone's life.

I owe a debt of gratitude to all who helped review varying drafts of this book. My parents have gone above and beyond in their help reviewing versions, as has my friend Phil Price. I will forever be in your debt for how much help you've given me.

I also cannot thank my parents enough for having brought me up to believe you can do and achieve whatever you want. Without them I would never have believed I could overcome the obstacles to travelling in the first place either. Now that I know it's possible I want to ensure as many other people as possible realise this, so they too can benefit from everything travelling gives you.

I also will be forever indebted to all those who have inspired me in my life and while writing this book, who motivated me to push for more and realise you don't have to accept normal.

My editor, Mary DeDanan, deserves special thanks for having improved this book immensely and for her tireless commitment to not letting me mess up my use of the English language too much. If you're in need of an editor, look her up at www.catchword.biz.

And last but by no means least I would like to thank all of the friends I've made on my travels. The people you meet when travelling make a huge difference to the experience you have and I couldn't have hoped for a better bunch of people to have crossed paths with. My travel friends have brought me hours of joy and inspiration, including a little push-start down the path of writing and kick up the arse when needed. In particular I'd like to thank all those who have been a part of making this particular trip so fun, even if we only met for 10 minutes: Blanche, Jen, Kathrin Missler, Andrea Rüd, Savanah Lily Watson, Zoé GalaxSea, Nadia Empez, Katharina Lehmann, EllBell Linares, Shell Bailey, Nino Amo, Lyncoln Amo, Claudia Uribe, Ilanna Gabriel, Celi Ramos, Amanda Mindy, Stephane Boghossian, Marisa Hansen, Liam Trieu, Whit Doig, Belal Nakhuda, Sasha Arora, Nikhil Sennik, Henry SF, Clio Evans, Ani Riedm, Johann Lindnmüllershausen, Fon Manotum , Elroy de Gans, Stephen D'Andrea, James Coyle, Salli Rutland, Denise Doherty, David HW, Corinne Hitching , Renita Kavallieros, Eduardo Cidade, Frederico Batista, Daniel Rocha, Laura- Maria Eviluoto, Victoria Bogrianova, Tatiana Sorokina, Rafael Cesar, Victor Corzo, Sophie Steenberg, Morgan Harteveld, Yoëlla van der Linden, Teuntje van Engelen, MJ Niki, Clem, Lewis Barnett, Alexander Thorin, Matilde Petersen, Russ Evans, Tomer Varsano, Frederic Heeg, Aidan Paringer, Sean Elmquist, Sofie Skou Seiersen, Signe Østerlund, Poh-Leng Devare, David Ribeiro, Stephanie Janette Gomes, Natacha Amione, Joshua Tustin, Willem Hegen, Charlotte Ward, Bryony Porter, Oli Millward, Brian Sigmon,

Edward de Roo, Arjun Thaker, Jace Sullivan, Klara Labesque, Marco Zeindler, Heather Cilinski, Harriet Baldwin, Bryony Roberts, Gisela Micaela, Clelia Teixeira, Fabian Schwarz, Siobán Morse, Culzean Kelly, Bennett Nadeau, Oscar Ramirez, Nick Sesno, Will Steger, Ali Peralta, Katrina Ikan, Sasha Newbold, Jhonny Vegeance, Kristin Schreiber, Neda Eff, Yudik Setyawan, Agung Dwintara, Jenny Farrah, Odin Zuhri, Felix Egnor, Pepe Silva, Wiro Basuki, Aji Muhidzir, Julio Valentino, Deano Scupham, JJ Goodman, Eitan Lev, Dedi Gun, Bobby , Samuel Harry, Filippo Villa, Bugy Elyan, Dodge Haruman, Alan Reşîd, Sakari McGregor, Alessandro Zibetti. Damien May, Mark Adato, Izaro Aro, Ainel Firas, Clemi Hardie, Lie Sel, Berlin Sihombing, Yurike Rahman, Adi Depedi, Sally Hellyer, Lorette Velting-Sibagariang, Sissi Soon, Senem Sönmez, Martin Moser, Johnny Partridge, Julianne Greco, Haney Wood, Fernando Daniel García Jiménez, Anni Purho, Kirby Bartlett, Adam Beith, Vilde Arnoy, Rodrigo Popoca, Rahime Acar, A-Gun Gunny, Yurike Rahman, Anja Mayer, Sarah Murray, Catherine Abonado, Thomy Maha Putra Dewa, John Jay , Mrks Rnld, Luke Chehab, Geir Pettersborg, Martina Machl, Harris Jackson, Daniel Potthoff, Christoph Maser, C-bee Miring, Andrew Stead, Lisa Jean-Mairet, Gusde Gautama, Mukhlis Bowele, Joni Jaguar, Tina May, Emilio Kuzma-Floyd, Matthew Della Bosca, Melissa Wharton, Sandra Hernandez, Nastasia Wong, Nick Riley, Jenna Johnson, Jessica Evans , Bryan Goldberg, Daniel Swinkels, Veronica Rooney, Darlene Branco, Michelle Halpern, Bronwyn Brown, Lisa Silva, Michelle Halpern, Charlotte Teague, Hannah Tobin, Sonia Rai, Vicky Coombs, Nick Teulon.

ACKNOWLEDGEMENTS

This is a long list of acknowledgements but I wanted to include very single one of you as so frequently people have a much bigger effect on our lives than they realise, even if it's just that they brightened up one day when we needed it most, and for that I want to thank all of you from the bottom of my heart. My trip wouldn't have been the same without you.

Printed in Great Britain
by Amazon